E-mail Addressing between Networks

E-mail, discussed in Chapter 5, is one of the most popular uses of the Internet. Use the address forms summarized below to exchange mail between the Internet and other popular networks.

BITNET: To send mail from a BITNET site to an Internet user, use one of the following address forms:

user@*host*

or

gateway!*domain*!*user*

To send mail from an Internet site to a BITNET user, use the following address form:

user%*site*.bitnet@*gateway*

(Substitute for *gateway* the name of a host that serves both Internet and BITNET.)

CompuServe: To send mail from a CompuServe site to an Internet user, use the following address form:

>Internet:*user*@*host*

(Add the prefix >Internet: to the Internet address.)

To send mail from an Internet user to a CompuServe site, use the following address form:

71234.567@compuserve.com

(Compuserve user IDs are two numbers separated by a comma. Replace the comma with a period and add the domain name compuserve.com.)

MCIMail: To send mail from an MCIMail site to an Internet user, use the following address form:

```
create <CR>
TO:   User Name
EMS:  Internet
MBX:  user@host.domain
```

To send mail from an Internet user to an MCIMail site, use one of the following address forms:

acctname@mci_mail.com

or

acct_id@mci_mail.com

(Account names may not be unique; MCI *acct ID* is a 7-digit number.)

Continues inside back cover.

For every kind of computer user, there is a SYBEX book.

All computer users learn in their own way. Some need straightforward and methodical explanations. Others are just too busy for this approach. But no matter what camp you fall into, SYBEX has a book that can help you get the most out of your computer and computer software while learning at your own pace.

Beginners generally want to start at the beginning. The **ABC's** series, with its step-by-step lessons in plain language, helps you build basic skills quickly. Or you might try our **Quick & Easy** series, the friendly, full-color guide.

The **Mastering** and **Understanding** series will tell you everything you need to know about a subject. They're perfect for intermediate and advanced computer users, yet they don't make the mistake of leaving beginners behind.

If you're a busy person and are already comfortable with computers, you can choose from two SYBEX series—**Up & Running** and **Running Start**. The **Up & Running** series gets you started in just 20 lessons. Or you can get two books in one, a step-by-step tutorial and an alphabetical reference, with our **Running Start** series.

Everyone who uses computer software can also use a computer software reference. SYBEX offers the gamut—from portable **Instant References** to comprehensive **Encyclopedias**, **Desktop References**, and **Bibles**.

SYBEX even offers special titles on subjects that don't neatly fit a category—like **Tips & Tricks**, the **Shareware Treasure Chests**, and a wide range of books for Macintosh computers and software.

SYBEX books are written by authors who are expert in their subjects. In fact, many make their living as professionals, consultants or teachers in the field of computer software. And their manuscripts are thoroughly reviewed by our technical and editorial staff for accuracy and ease-of-use.

So when you want answers about computers or any popular software package, just help yourself to SYBEX.

For a complete catalog of our publications, please write:

SYBEX Inc.
2021 Challenger Drive
Alameda, CA 94501
Tel: (510) 523-8233/(800) 227-2346 Telex: 336311
Fax: (510) 523-2373

SYBEX is committed to using natural resources wisely to preserve and improve our environment. As a leader in the computer book publishing industry, we are aware that over 40% of America's solid waste is paper. This is why we have been printing the text of books like this one on recycled paper since 1982.

This year our use of recycled paper will result in the saving of more than 15,300 trees. We will lower air pollution effluents by 54,000 pounds, save 6,300,000 gallons of water, and reduce landfill by 2,700 cubic yards.

In choosing a SYBEX book you are not only making a choice for the best in skills and information, you are also choosing to enhance the quality of life for all of us.

THE
INTERNET
ROADMAP

THE
INTERNET
ROADMAP

Bennett Falk

SYBEX®

San Francisco • Paris • Düsseldorf • Soest

Acquisitions Editor: David Clark
Developmental Editor: David Peal
Editor: James A. Compton
Technical Editor: Erik Ingenito
Book Designer: Helen Bruno
Technical Art: Cuong Le
Page Layout and Typesetting: Len Gilbert
Proofreader/Production Assistant: Janet Boone
Indexer: Ted Laux
Cover Designer: Ingalls + Associates
Cover Illustrator: Robert Kopecky

SYBEX is a registered trademark of SYBEX Inc.

Library of Congress Card Number: 93-85743
ISBN: 0-7821-1365-6

Manufactured in the United States of America
10 9 8 7 6 5

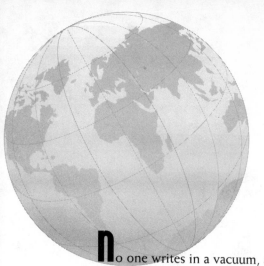

Acknowledgments

No one writes in a vacuum, and even a short book like this one has a complicated social heritage. You would not be reading this now if it were not for the efforts of many people, and I am grateful to all the friends and associates who helped this project on to completion.

Special thanks should go to Mary Eisenhart, the editor of *Micro-Times* and a great friend, for her constant encouragement, and for making this project possible in the first place.

At SYBEX, Jim Compton and David Peal contributed much more than the editorial sensibilities their jobs require. I thank them for their unfailing support and patience.

This project was begun during sabbatical leave from Sybase. Taylor Pohlman, Lou Muggeo, and Bob Cornelis of Sybase Technical Support were very generous in their encouragement and made adjustments in my work schedule so the book could be completed.

Robin Clark and George Martin of Onyx Pharmaceuticals very kindly shared their network knowledge and Internet experience. Many friends contributed encouragement and played the part of test audience. Thanks especially to Margaret Campbell, Nick Cuccia, David Hawkins, Sarah Satterlee, and Mark Theodoropolous.

Thanks above all to Margaret Moreland.

AT A GLANCE

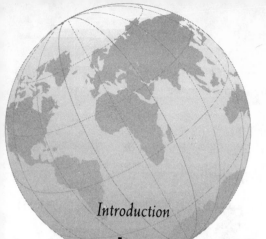

Table of Contents

part three THE INTERNET COMMUNITY'S APPLICATIONS: GOPHER, WORLDWIDEWEB, AND USENET

appendices

Introduction

This book introduces the basics of working with the Internet. You'll learn what the Internet is and how to use its essential applications or programs. Along the way, you'll be introduced to some key information resources that you can use as the starting point for exploring the Internet further. You'll soon find that the Internet doesn't stand still, but the topics covered here will give you everything you need to get started with the Internet as it is now and to grow with it as new applications and resources are introduced.

What You Need to Know Before You Start

About all that's needed for you to get something out of this book is some degree of comfort with using some sort of computer. Exactly what sort of computer you're comfortable with doesn't really matter: you'll find something familiar on virtually every computer you work with on the Internet.

What does "some degree of comfort" mean? Basically, there are three skills that will be helpful to anyone reading this book. First, you should know in general what files, disks, and directories (or folders) are, and you should know how to do things with files, disks, and directories—how to move a file from one disk to another, how to move around in a hierarchy of directories, how to take a file from one directory and put it into another, and the like. A second helpful skill is being able to tell the difference between the application programs that you use to do the work you're interested in and the operating system that runs on your computer. This boils down to being aware of what commands to issue when. (Typing the operating system command "dir" when you're running a word processor is unlikely to produce a directory listing.) Finally, it is helpful if you've had some experience using your computer to talk to a modem.

There are a few things you *don't* have to know before reading this book. Knowledge of the UNIX operating system is not required. Computers running UNIX *are* common on the Internet, and knowing UNIX is a good thing; but it is hardly a prerequisite for being able to do things on the Internet. (See also Appendix D, "Just Enough UNIX," for general information about UNIX.)

Knowing how networks work isn't required either. In general, explaining in detail how networks work is outside the scope of this book. It's a good thing to know, but you can become quite proficient at using network resources without understanding the technical details of what's going on.

How to Read This Book

This book has three parts and four short appendices. In Part One, we'll discuss what the Internet really is, concentrating on three components: the physical network (the cabling that holds the Internet together), protocols (the tools that get messages from one place to another), and network applications (the programs that put you in touch with the network). We will also step through a simple Internet program named finger and introduce some tools to help you get oriented on the network. Read the chapters in Part One if you're interested in how the

Internet works. Any user can work smarter and faster by under-standing the framework of the Internet. Understanding this frame-work is especially important because it is the part of the Internet that, amid the system's rapid growth, changes the least.

Part Two discusses ftp, telnet, and electronic mail. These are "atomic" network applications: they are more or less universally available, and they are building blocks for many Internet services. Read the chapters in Part Two if you are trying to locate or retrieve specific data, or trying to communicate with a specific person or group of people. Just about every Internet user needs to know some-thing about ftp, telnet, and e-mail.

Part Three presents contributions from the Internet user commu-nity. User-developed applications (like gopher and the World-WideWeb) provide a simpler interface for Internet resources. The most visible contributions from the Internet community are in the USENET News, an immense bulletin board that serves as a forum in which literally thousands of topics are discussed. Read Part Three if you need quick access to the more popular data sources. You'll learn to use global search tools that truly put the world at your fingertips.

The appendices contain practical information about a number of topics.

The Internet Roadmap is almost a random-access book. Like any road-map, it has more than one starting point and more than one destination. That's why Chapter 2 shows you how to find out "where you are" on the Internet—your address and the tools available to you. Beyond that, you can read the other chapters in whatever order works best for you. If you want to send e-mail to a friend, start with Chapter 5. If you're impatient to start doing things right away, begin with gopher in Chapter 6—it's the closest the Internet comes to being user-friendly. Wherever you start, enjoy the trip and don't forget to write:

roadmap@sybex.com

PART ONE

INTRODUCING

THE

INTERNET

The two chapters in Part I provide a general orientation to what the Internet is and how it works. Chapter 1 discusses three of the Internet's essential components: the cabling that holds the Internet together, the network protocols that get messages from place to place on the Internet, and the client/server architecture that you'll encounter in programs that use the Internet. Along the way, you'll also be introduced to the `finger` program and some of the information resources it can be used to reach. Chapter 2 shows you how to discover some things about the computer that provides your point of contact with the Internet. You'll learn about `ping` and other programs you can use to watch the Internet in action. You'll learn how to identify the computer you work with, and how to tell if it's connected to the Internet.

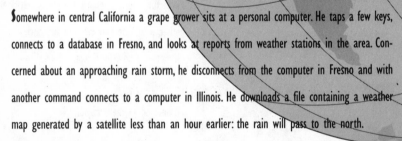

What Is
the Internet?

Somewhere in central California a grape grower sits at a personal computer. He taps a few keys, connects to a database in Fresno, and looks at reports from weather stations in the area. Concerned about an approaching rain storm, he disconnects from the computer in Fresno and with another command connects to a computer in Illinois. He downloads a file containing a weather map generated by a satellite less than an hour earlier: the rain will pass to the north.

- Two hundred miles north, in Sacramento, the manager of a produce store consults a different database, also on the Fresno computer, that tracks the pricing and supply of grapes from California, Arizona, and Mexico. The Arizona supplies are very low, and the price difference between the

imported and California grapes isn't enough to justify the longer shipment. He picks up the phone and places an order.

- In an industrial park two blocks away, a molecular biologist at a small biotechnology company puts the finishing touches on documentation for a patent application and sends it via electronic mail to the company's Vice President for Research and Development in Seattle and to their patent attorney in Washington, DC. She sits back to relax, pulls a bunch of grapes from her lunch sack and checks the weather maps from the computer in Illinois. "Hey, it looks like it's gonna rain," she remarks to no one in particular. A co-worker shakes his head and throws open the door of the windowless room. Raindrops splatter against the window across the hall.

- Seconds later the patent documentation arrives in the attorney's on-line mailbox. He skims through the text, forwards a copy to a clerk and saves the message for his own use. Something in it piques his curiosity. He makes a few quick movements with his workstation's mouse. A menu appears in a new window on the screen, and he positions the pointer on the "US Patents" item to begin a keyword search through recent patents.

- The Vice President for R & D did not notice the electronic mail when it arrived. He was sipping grape juice from a plastic carton and staring intently at his screen hoping to discover the melting point of tungsten. The question had appeared in a network scavenger hunt game he played occasionally. He never scored well, but at least he had something to talk about when he ran into members of the computer group.

- All these people are using the Internet, a global network of computer networks that is both a medium for communication and reference resource on virtually any subject.

A View of the Internet from 30,000 Feet

The Internet was established roughly a quarter-century ago to meet the needs of researchers working in the defense industry in the United States. It gradually outgrew the defense industry to become a truly global network and an indispensable tool for academic research in all fields. It continues to grow, now spilling out of the academic world to offer both information access and a fast, inexpensive means of communication to the general public. It will be the next public utility.

The Internet is the world's largest computer network, but there is no easy way to characterize just how large it is. An estimated 1.2 million computers were connected to the Internet at the beginning of 1993. However, the Internet doesn't reckon its membership in either computers or computer users. The Internet's constituents are networks. Today over 12,000 local networks are connected to the Internet, and its rate of growth is steadily increasing. In May of 1993, over 1000 new networks joined the Internet. Nor do new networks account for all the Internet's growth. The Internet's audience expands with every new computer or user that is added to any of its constituent networks.

Test Drive–Getting Your Hands On the Internet

The purpose of this chapter is to give you a solid foundation in the concepts underlying the Internet. The few minutes you spend now learning about the physical cabling, the protocols, and the software that the Internet consists of will make you a smarter, more efficient user down the road. But if you're like most of us, you're probably wondering when you can get behind the wheel and take it out for a test drive. So before we get started with the theory, let's take a moment for some Internet practice.

To use the Internet you have to be working with a computer that is connected to it. This could be a PC, a Macintosh, or a multiuser system (UNIX-based, for example). If you're on a multiuser computer, you'll have to log in before you can execute commands. (See Appendix C for information about logging in.) If you're using a personal computer that's attached to the Internet, you probably won't have to go through a login procedure.

A Simple Command: finger

Once you've logged in, you can execute commands that use your computer's Internet connection. Of all the commands that access the Internet, the easiest to use is finger. This command displays information about a user. To execute it, just type the word finger followed by the name of the user you want to know about:

```
% finger bennett
Login name: bennett       In real life: Bennett Falk
Directory: /usr/u/bennett Shell: /bin/csh
On since Jul 18 15:29:13 on ttyp2 from optimism
23 seconds Idle Time
No unread mail
No Plan.
```

In addition to such standard items as the user's name and home directory, finger also displays the contents of a file named .plan if there is such a file in the user's home directory. (The No Plan message in the example indicates that there is no .plan file for the user bennett.) You can put anything you like in your .plan file, and as you'll see shortly, many Internet users use their `.plan` files creatively. If you have a user name on the computer you use, try executing the `finger` command using that name. If `finger` prints a message similar to the output above, you're ready to proceed. Your command may return a message like

```
finger: Command not found.
```

This means that the `finger` command is not available to you. That's a serious impediment, but it's hardly the end of the world. See the accompanying sidebar for hints on coping with this.

 WHEN FINGER IS FICKLE - - - - - - - - - - - - - -

There are three unusual conditions you might encounter when you try to execute the `finger` command.

1. Finger can't find the user: If you provide the name of a nonexistent user, `finger` will respond this way:

```
finger etaoin          'etaoin' is a mistyped user name.
Login name: etaoin              In real life: ???
```

2. Finger can't find the computer: If `finger` can't interpret the computer name you've given it, it will respond in this way:

```
finger bennett@shrdlu.com
unknown host: shrdlu.com
```

This can be caused by mistyping the computer name when entering the command. If so, execute the command with the correct name. If you've typed the name correctly and still receive the "unknown host" message, your computer's connection to the Internet may be faulty (or the computer may not be attached to the Internet at all). Ask the system administrator for help.

3. Your computer can't find finger: Finally, you may get this response:

```
finger aurora@xi.uleth.ca
finger:  Command not found.
```

This means that your computer can't find the finger command to execute it. The finger command is widespread, but not ubiquitous. There is a way to work around this using the telnet command. The name you supply to finger has the format user@computer.name. If your computer can't find the finger command, try telnet with the computer name and the number 79. If telnet connects successfully, type the user name and press Return, as in this example:

```
telnet xi.uleth.ca 79
Trying...
Connected to xi.uleth.ca.
Escape character is '^]'.
aurora
Login name: aurora              In real life: Aurora Finger
Directory: /userfiles/others/oler/solar/aurora     Shell: /bin/true
Never logged in.
Plan:
=============================================
S.T.D. HOURLY AURORAL ACTIVITY STATUS REPORT
=============================================
---<Output Truncated>---
```

It is possible that you will get a "Command not found" message in response to your telnet command as well. If this happens, you should confirm with the computer's administrator that it really is connected to the Internet.

A Finger on the Internet's Pulse

If you were able to execute the `finger` command using your own user name, you're ready to do a simple test of your computer's Internet access. The command you'll use is

```
finger quake@geophys.washington.edu
```

Be sure to spell everything correctly and to place punctuation marks just as shown. If your computer is really connected to the Internet, this command will `finger` a user named `quake` at a computer named `geophys.washington.edu`. When you execute this command, it will return, in addition to the expected user information, a summary of recent earthquake activity similar to that shown in Listing 1.1. The `.plan` file for `quake` contains information about seismic events. To display this file, your `finger` command makes a connection to a computer in the Geophysics Department of the University of Washington.

Congratulations, you're using the Internet.

listing 1.1:
Using finger to Access the Earthquake Information Service
– – – – –

```
finger quake.geophys.washington.edu
Login name: quake      In real life: Earthquake Information
Directory: /uO/quake      Shell: /uO/quake/run_quake
Last login Thu Jul 15 21:23 on ttyi2

Plan:
Information about Recent earthquakes are reported here for public use.
Catalogs are available by anonymous ftp in
geophys.washington.edu:pub/seis-net

--<Informational message truncated>--

Recent events reported by the USGS National Earthquake Information
Center
  DATE-TIME (UT)  LAT     LON     DEP   MAG       LOCATION AREA
  93/07/12 14:45  43.5N   139.4E   33   6.0    EASTERN SEA OF JAPAN
```

```
93/07/12 16:01   43.0N   139.5E    33   5.9    EASTERN SEA OF JAPAN
93/07/14 12:31   38.4N    21.6E    33   5.4    GREECE
--<output truncated>--
```

The Earthquake Information Service maintained by the University of Washington is one of many information resources accessible via the `finger` command. Here are a few of the other services that can be reached with `finger`:

- Earthquake information:

  ```
  finger quake@geophys.washington.edu
  ```

- News from NASA:

  ```
  finger nasanews@space.mit.edu
  ```

  Solar activity:

  ```
  finger aurora@xi.uleth.ca
  finger solar@xi.uleth.ca
  finger daily@xi.uleth.ca
  ```

  Tropical storm statistics:

  ```
  finger forecast@typhoon.atmos.colostate.edu
  ```

A Closer View of the Internet

Describing the Internet can be daunting. A network as big and as interconnected as the Internet can seem chaotic, like a cloud of connected networks. Describing what you *do* on the Internet is no easier. To say that the Internet provides information access and communication does not begin to convey the breadth of what it offers.

In spite of its size and diversity, however, there are three fundamental elements that make the Internet work, and these parts fill the same roles regardless of the network's size or the uses to which it is put. Understanding these essential components will make the Internet easier to use and give you an advantage in adapting to new developments and responding to problems.

The first component is a physical network. The Internet behaves as though all the computers in all the participating networks were joined by a giant cable. In fact, all the computers on the Internet *are* joined by connectors (cables) of various kinds. As we will see, many features of the Internet can be attributed directly to this physical network, the cabling that holds it all together.

The cabling, however, is only a starting point. The cable carries network traffic, but it doesn't make the traffic meaningful. One step away from the bare cable, we will encounter a number of specialized languages for transmitting messages (not unlike the street addresses and zip codes used by the postal service). These languages are *protocols*, and they divvy up the physical network into discreet locations and enable one location to send messages to another.

Finally, neither the cable nor the network protocols are things that human beings directly interact with. Most of what you will see when you use the network are software tools or applications. But network applications are different from single-user applications on stand-alone computers. The distinguishing feature of a network application is its structure or architecture, and it is not possible to do justice to the Internet without talking about network applications.

The Tao of Cable

Considered as a piece of cable, the Internet is like a very long string to which millions of tin cans are attached. (The Tin Can Network is shown in Figure 1.1.) Well over a million computers participate in the Internet, and they are all held together by cabling very much like a tin can network would be. The Internet's physical network functions like an immense, single circuit, a giant party line that carries everyone's data.

More than any other component, the cabling defines the network. In one way or another, all of the following are defined primarily in relation to the physical network:

- What it means to have an Internet connection.

- What the network's performance will be like.

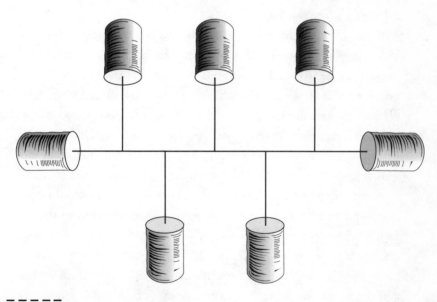

- - - - -
figure 1.1 The Tin Can Network.

- What the costs are.

- Who has the right to make policy about the acceptable uses of the network.

It's All Connected

You get access to Internet by using a computer that is connected to the physical network. Computers connected to the Internet are said to *host* the network, and the phrase *network host* simply means a computer connected to the physical network. We will use *hosts* and *computers* interchangeably. The network cabling itself doesn't really care what sorts of computers are connected to it. You are likely to communicate with computers of all sorts (supercomputers, massively parallel computers, mainframes, supermicros, and personal computers) on the Internet, but none of them will perform any better than the cable that gives you access .

If you have a personal login account with a commercial Internet access provider, you probably use a modem to call a computer connected to the Internet, as illustrated in Figure 1.2. The speed at which you exchange information with the network is limited by the telephone line and the speed of your modem. The phone connection you use to access a computer on the Internet is at best a temporary extension of the physical network. The physical network really begins at the computer that you've connected to.

Attaching a computer to the Internet is usually a matter of connecting it to a local network that is, in turn, connected to the Internet. There are privately owned local networks in businesses and on campuses everywhere. If the local network where you work is connected to the Internet, you have Internet access through the computer you use on that network. Local networks are commonly held together by cabling that can provide excellent service over

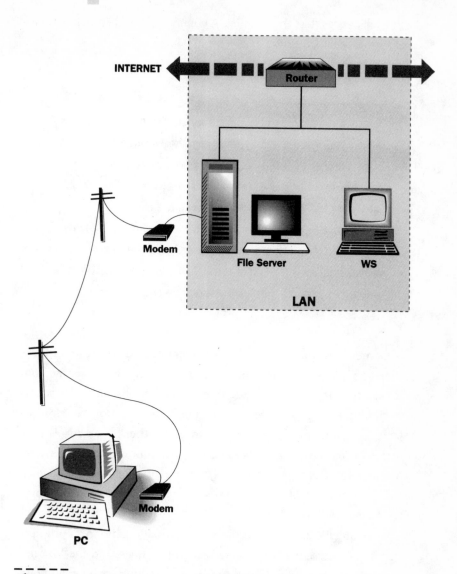

<u>fi𝘨ure 1.2</u> Connecting to the Internet Via Modem

short distances (less than a mile). A common physical medium for local networks is Ethernet.

✖ TIP

If you use a workstation on an Ethernet-based LAN, the Ethernet connection is
either a small, metal "T" with a cable running through it attached to the back
of the computer or a small plastic box (containing a transceiver) with a few
lights blinking red or green or amber attached to the computer by a modular
cable. If you work at a computer that is attached to a LAN, be extremely
careful around the physical connector. Ethernet transceivers can easily find their
way underfoot to be stepped on or tripped over. Detaching an Ethernet
connection improperly can interrupt network service across the entire LAN. In
general, it's a good idea to leave maintenance of the physical LAN connection to
your network administrators.

Somewhere on any local network connected to the Internet is
a *router*, a computer that bridges the gap between whatever medium
is used for the LAN and the long-distance line that provides access
to the Internet at large, as illustrated in Figure 1.3. The router insu-
lates the LAN and the Internet from each other. The LAN is protected from having to process a large volume of network traffic
destined for sites outside the LAN, and the Internet is protected from
the interruptions of service (crashes) that are the lot of local networks everywhere.

The long distance (or wide area) portions of the Internet's physical
network are essentially dedicated telephone lines, and the Internet
cannot currently be extended to places that don't have a telephone
line network adequate for data transmission. Parts of eastern Europe,
Africa, and Asia (or any place where the telephone system is not

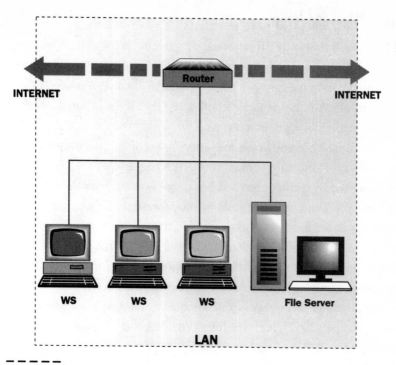

figure 1.3 A Local Network Connected to the Internet

highly developed) will have fewer and slower Internet connections than, for example, the United States, France, and Japan.

The lines that carry Internet traffic differ from the phone lines that carry voice traffic in two important ways. They tend to be point-to-point lines (which means that the circuit is always open between the two points the line connects), and they have a greater capacity for carrying data than the lines that make up the network to which your home phone is attached.

The Speed of Ones and Zeros

There was a time when the fastest way to move a lot of information from one place to another sixty miles away was load a station wagon with magnetic tape and drive for an hour. When data moves from place to place, it moves at a certain speed that is determined largely by the medium over which it travels.

The capacity of any line is measured in bits of data transmitted per second. (Bit is short for "binary digit." It is the smallest unit of information used by a computer, and has only two possible values: 0 and 1. Typically, computers use eight bits to represent a single character.) Ethernet-based local networks currently transmit data at speeds up to 10 million bits per second (or 10 Mbps) over distances up to one kilometer. This rate translates to roughly 1.2 million characters, nearly six hundred screenfuls of information, per second.

Building a global network one kilometer at a time would be tedious and expensive. Telephone lines provide good long distance coverage and a choice of transmission speeds. Voice-grade phone lines like the one your modem uses can transmit data at speeds up to 19,200 bits per second or 19.2 kbps (kilobits per second). This works out to a little more than a screenful of data (25 lines by 80 characters per line)—much slower than Ethernet.

Beyond voice grade lines, there are "leased" lines: dedicated phone lines between two points. Leased lines are capable of carrying data at rates between 56 and 64 kbps. The lines connecting the first four sites on the Internet's precursor, ARPANET, more than twenty years ago carried data at 56 kbps (about 3.5 screens of information per second).

The demand for higher capacity lines has produced the service grades that are commonly used in wide area networking in North America. T1 lines, widely used as major data arteries, have a capacity of 1.5 million bits per second (Mbps) or 94 screens of data per second. T3 grade lines transmit data at thirty times that rate (45 Mbps or just over 2800 screensful per second). T3 lines were first introduced to the Internet in 1991 and are currently used throughout the Internet's North American backbone. A map of the T3 backbone is shown in Figure 1.4.

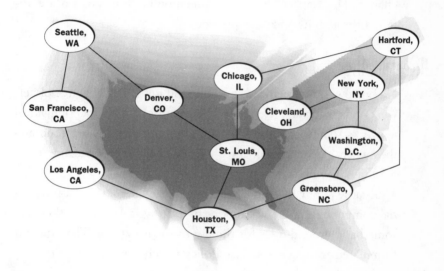

figure 1.4 North American T3 Backbone

Paying for the Internet

Cabling is not free. And while it is usually clear who pays for and owns a local network, it is not always clear who should bear the cost of installing and maintaining the long distance connections that make the Internet a worldwide system. The cost of connecting a local network to the Internet is usually paid by whoever owns the local network. That owner negotiates a connection with a site already connected to the Internet and pays for the dedicated line that connects the local network to the Internet site. Commercial Internet access providers usually pass their costs back to their subscribers through monthly charges or hourly usage fees.

The T3 backbone mentioned above is a critical piece of the network in North America, and its maintenance has not been left to chance. The National Science Foundation funds this part of the Internet through its NSFNET project.

Acceptable Use

No one owns the Internet as a whole, and it is remarkably free of network-wide regulation. Certainly all the parts of the Internet (individual networks, some local and some quite large) are owned by someone, and the owners of local networks set policies for the appropriate use of the resources they make available to the larger community.

Because public funds maintain one of the Internet's most substantial components, the T3 backbone of the physical network, there are some basic ground rules for the use of the backbone. The NSF has formulated an Acceptable Use Policy which applies to traffic using the NSFNET facilities on the network.

The NSFNET Acceptable Use Policy gives us a view of the network as a tool for education and academic research. The policy advocates the use of the Internet for things like communications between researchers, collecting information about and applying for grants and research contracts, and administering of research programs and academic professional societies (referred to as "disciplinary societies").

Some kinds of commercial activity (advertising, consulting for pay, general use by "for-profit" institutions) are declared to be unacceptable. Most of the vignettes at the beginning of this chapter describe common uses of the Internet that are, strictly speaking, unacceptable under the NSFNET policy.

However, the Internet is rapidly changing. The commercial sector is the fastest growing portion of the Internet user community, and many of the large regional networks that make up the Internet have acceptable-use policies that are far less restrictive of commercial activities than the NSFNET policy. Gradually, an infrastructure to support commercial use of the Internet is being built alongside the structure that protects the interests of the academic community.

Quite apart from acceptable-use policies, there is a general consensus among Internet users about the proper use of the Internet. The network is a cooperative venture, and you should not do anything that would place at risk the network, its users, or the agencies that contribute resources to the Internet.

✖ TIP

Check with your Internet access provider for the use policy that governs the local network. You should also ask the access provider about NSFNET backbone access and your obligation to abide by the NSF Acceptable Use Policy.

The Dance of Protocols

Of course, no one thinks that it's particularly difficult to use a piece of cable, no matter how large: you simply pull the string tight and shout into the tin can attached to it. The use of cabling doesn't ordinarily require a manual.

Communicating through a medium as complex as the Internet, however, raises some issues that never occur to two people trying to talk into tin cans joined by a piece of string. Imagine for a moment the effect of a million talkers on the tin can network with a single string carrying everyone's speech to all the attached cans. The jumble of noise coming over the network would make it virtually impossible for anyone to find a partner in dialogue.

A monitor attached directly to a part of the Internet's physical network would show something similar to the cacophony of voice traffic over string. You would see a jumble of messages going to and from nearby sites, possibly interspersed with messages (irrelevant to any local site) on their way from one distant place to another.

Unlike the tin can network, however, partners in dialogue over the Internet routinely do find each other. Messages travel long distances, intact, without distortion or delay. The component of the network that makes this possible is a collection of *protocols* that handle different aspects of delivering messages from one place to another. A protocol is a mutually agreed-upon format or set of conventions, defined for a specific purpose. Some protocols choreograph the movement of messages, some check the integrity of what was sent, and some "massage" data from one format into another.

The use of protocols is certainly not unique to computer networks. For example, the familiar act of addressing an envelope to be put in the mail exercises at least one protocol. The address and return address on an envelope are messages to the post office describing where the letter is to go under various circumstances. These messages must appear in their expected places on the envelope and must use a format the postal service understands if the envelope is to be deliverable.

Protocols on the Internet

Protocols do their work behind the scenes. The task of translating messages into and out of protocols is handled silently by network hosts, and human users are spared the drudgery of addressing by hand the individual packets that cross the network. Every message transmitted over the Internet passes through at least three different levels of protocol: a *network protocol* to oversee getting messages from place to place, a *transport protocol* to manage the integrity of what is transmitted, and an *application protocol* that turns the network transmission into something we can recognize as the answer to a request that we dispatched through a network application. These protocols are nested or layered very much like the boxes in Figure 1.5.

The protocol used by the Internet for getting messages from one machine to another is called the Internet Protocol (IP). The Internet Protocol is a *network protocol*, and its job is to manage the logistics of getting a message from the sending machine to the receiving machine.

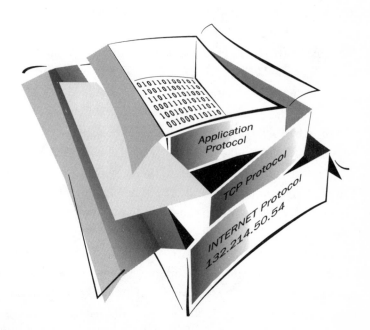

figure 1.5 The Layering of Protocols.

Messages delivered by the Internet protocol are called *packets*, and these are quite small, usually fifteen hundred bytes or fewer. Since this is much smaller than many of the messages and files that are transmitted over the Internet, it is common for a transmission to require multiple packets.

Collecting related packets, putting them in the proper order, and verifying that none are garbled are tasks outside the scope of the Internet Protocol itself. (They are handled by yet another protocol that works with network transmissions on a larger scale.)

The protocols that deal with the integrity of network transmissions (particularly those that span multiple packets) are *transport protocols*: the Transmission Control Protocol (TCP) and the User Datagram Protocol.

Finally, there are application protocols that take care of formatting requests formulated by users and the data that returns in response to those requests. There are about as many application protocols as there are applications on the Internet. Mail, `telnet`, `ftp`, `archie`, `gopher`, WAIS, and WorldWideWeb—you'll learn about using these applications later in this book—each has its own protocol.

The Internet Protocol and the Transmission Control Protocol are paired so frequently that it is common to speak of TCP/IP networks. For years, TCP/IP has been the protocol of choice among UNIX vendors, and there are several TCP/IP implementations for Macintosh and PC class computers as well as for other multiuser computers. The use of the TCP/IP protocol suite is widespread outside the Internet: simply running TCP/IP does not guarantee an Internet connection.

From a user's perspective, any TCP/IP-based local area network is like a miniature version of the Internet. Many of the tools available on the Internet (`mail`, `telnet`, and `ftp`) are packaged with the basic networking software on UNIX systems. Applications developed by the Internet community could also be moved to a TCP/IP-based

LAN, and there is no reason why an Internet application such as gopher could not be used to manage local resources.

Internet Addresses

For the Internet Protocol to do its job, there must be some way to identify the places or sites that will exchange messages. The physical network, the cable, is largely undifferentiated. Computers are attached to it at various points, but the points of attachment are arbitrary and changeable. Under the Internet Protocol, each network and each computer attached to the physical network has a fixed address that allows any other computer to reach it even if the physical location of the computer changes.

An Internet address is a 32 bit-number, just the sort of thing computers were invented to deal with. To make things easier on the human beings who occasionally need to read these numbers, Internet addresses are usually written as four numbers separated by periods:

130.214.50.59

Each number represents eight bits of the Internet address. (This fact is largely insignificant, but it does mean that none of the four numbers can be larger than 255.)

The 32-bit IP address has two components. One identifies the individual computer, and the other identifies the network of which that computer is a member. The network component is assigned when the local network registers for an Internet connection with the Internet Network Information Center (InterNIC, also known as "the NIC"). The InterNIC supplies the portion of the address that identifies the local network and gives the local network's administrator a range of addresses that can be assigned to individual hosts within the local network.

An Internet address is a powerful thing. It uniquely identifies a host on the Internet, and it is the key to interacting with that computer and any applications installed. For example, some of the weather reports used by farmers are on a host whose address is `129.8.100.15`. Using the command `telnet 129.8.100.15`, you can connect to the computer at this addresss and use the database. Although you can reach many of the information resources available on the Internet through menu systems, many others will be identified only by IP address, so it's a good idea to become comfortable with these numbers.

Numbers Are Not Enough: The Domain Naming System

An IP address uniquely identifies a host on the Internet, but even in its human-readable format (four numbers separated by periods) an IP address can be hard to work with. The numeric addresses don't have much personality, and are difficult to remember. The IP address `128.114.143.4` isn't particularly memorable, but you won't quickly forget the name `infoslug` (which refers to the computer at that address). The one-to-one correspondence of IP addresses and computers doesn't provide the flexibility that is sometimes needed in managing the placement of resources on the Internet.

Because each IP address refers to one and only one network host, it has been relatively easy to identify network hosts by name as well as by number. A well-defined set of conventions for naming computers on the network has evolved along with a directory service for looking up names. These conventions and the directory service are known collectively as the Domain Name System (DNS). A *domain* is just a named group of network hosts, and you can get a good picture of where a computer on the network is if you know its name (host name) and the domains it belongs to.

NOTE

The local network administrator is responsible for establishing local domains and registering them with the NIC, which maintains a database of domains and their members. This process is similar to network registration, but the two are completely independent of each other: registering a network does not automatically create a domain for that network. Some sites register domain names well before they have Internet access, to simplify the exchange of electronic mail between the site and the Internet.

Domain-style names consist of a series of names separated by periods. A Fully Qualified Domain Name (FQDN for those who require acronyms) represents the name of a computer and the hierarchy of domains in which it is nested. An FQDN looks a little like an IP address, but there is no correspondence between the fields in the two names. The fully qualified domain name for the computer that contains the agricultural database consulted above looks like this:

```
caticsuf.csufresno.edu
```

We can use this name in place of an IP address. The command `telnet caticsuf.csufresno.edu` would connect us to the computer that maintains the agricultural database.

Let's dissect this name. The leftmost field of the name (*caticsuf*) is the host name, the name assigned to the computer by its administrator. Following the host name are names of domains the host belongs to in order of increasing generality. The computer named `caticsuf` is a member of the `csufresno` domain (a domain at California State University in Fresno) which in turn is a member of the `edu` domain—

the domain for educational institutions.

The name `caticsuf.csufresno.edu` is an *organizational* domain name: it tells us what sort of organization the named computer belongs to. As listed in Table 1.1, there are seven top-level organizational domains in the Internet's hierarchy, and every computer that registers an organizational name must fit in one of these top-level domains.

There are also top-level domains that are geographically-based. These domains (listed in Table 1.2) have two-letter names representing country. The lower level domains beneath the "country-based" domains are a mixture of geographical and non-geographical names. For example, the name `well.sf.ca.us` indicates that the computer named `well` is in the San Francisco area, in California, in the United States. On the other hand, `info.anu.edu.au` identifies the host named `info` at the Australian National University, an educational institution, in Australia. Note that the geographical codes are unique only within fields, not across them. For example, Canada's country code is `ca`. California's state code is also `ca`.

table 1.1: Top-Level Organizational Domains.

DOMAIN NAME	CATEGORY
com	Commercial Organizations
edu	Educational Institutions
gov	U.S. Government Organizations
int	International Organizations
mil	U.S. Military Organizations
net	Network Backbone Systems and Information Centers
org	Nonprofit Organizations

table 1.2: Top-Level Geographical Domains.

DOMAIN NAME	CATEGORY
au	Australia
at	Austria
ca	Canada
cl	Chile
dk	Denmark
ec	Ecuador
fi	Finland
fr	France
de	Germany
is	Iceland
it	Italy
jp	Japan
kr	Korea
nz	New Zealand
es	Spain
se	Sweden
tw	Taiwan
uk	UK/Ireland
us	United States

NOTE

Whenever you refer to a host on the Internet by name, the software you're using will translate the name into an IP Address and use that. This translation always starts with the most general domain. Consequently, the rightmost field in a domain name is always assumed to be a top-level domain: either one of the organization types or a country code. A reference to well.sf.ca will be assumed to be a computer in Canada, and the translation will fail. To be translatable, domain names must always end with the name of a top-level domain.

A CLOSER LOOK AT THE FINGER COMMAND — — — — — —

Now that you're familiar with domain names, we can make a little more sense of the finger commands listed for NASA and weather information in our opening exercise. Remember that a finger command looks like this:

```
finger user@computer
```

To finger a user elsewhere on the Internet, the computer name (everything to the right of the "@") should be in domain name format. When you finger solar@xi.uleth.ca, for example, you're querying a computer named xi at the University of Lethbridge (uleth) in Canada (ca). Notice that some of the names have more fields than others. The tropical storm forecasting service is located on the host named typhoon in a local domain named atmos at Colorado State University (colostate) which is in the top-level edu domain.

On the Internet a host is known by an IP address, but it may have several names (all of which map to its IP address). Unlike IP addresses, names can be reassigned or reused, and this makes them more versatile than IP addresses.

When, for example, the agricultural database at Cal State Fresno outgrows the computer it's on, it will be moved to a different computer, with a different IP address. If you use the old computer's IP address, you will be routed to that computer and there will be no database there. However, when the database is moved, the administrator of the local network at Cal State Fresno will be able to reassign the name (caticsuf.csufresno.edu) so that it refers to the IP address of the new computer. References to the name will then be routed automatically to the new computer.

Using Protocols to Extend the Physical Network: SLIP and PPP

You may have realized that since the Internet Protocol runs throughout the Internet, it must be usable across many different kinds of cable. The design of the protocol is such that it can be used with physical networks of many different media, everything from slow leased lines to high speed-fiber optics.

Technological improvements have reduced the cost of high-speed (9600 bps and above) modems, and it is common for networking software packages to include software to run the Internet Protocol over voice-grade phone lines. The advent of the Serial Line Internet Protocol (SLIP) and the Point-to-Point Protocol (PPP) makes it possible for anyone with a computer, a modem, and a phone line to connect directly to the Internet.

This is a different service from simply being able to log in to a computer that is attached to the Internet. If, for example, you dial in to an Internet host from a personal computer, log in to your account and work with the Internet, your personal computer is completely unknown to the Internet.

With SLIP and PPP, however, your personal computer can become an Internet host in its own right with a unique IP address. Your personal computer will still use a dial-in connection to an Internet host, but with SLIP or PPP your computer interacts with the Internet using the Internet Protocol, and this allows you to run on your own computer applications that connect directly to resources throughout the Internet.

From a user perspective, SLIP and PPP do essentially the same thing. SLIP is the older of the two protocols, and there are a number of products on the market and in the public domain that use it. SLIP is not very sophisticated: it exchanges IP packets over a serial line with a minimum of error checking and additional encoding. This means that a SLIP connection will have very little overhead (it adds only one byte to the IP packet), but may have problems coping with the line noise and other interruptions that are common on serial lines.

PPP is more versatile. It has much more robust message control, and it is designed to handle protocols other than IP. However, it also imposes more overhead on the transmission. PPP will be standardized in a way that SLIP was not (that is, there will be a standard specifying how PPP works). In the long run, PPP should render SLIP obsolete.

The advantage of SLIP or PPP connections is that you can run applications that use the Internet on computers that don't have a permanent network connection of any sort. (Most computers running Internet applications are not stand-alone computers: they are on a LAN of some sort.) If your Internet access comes from a commercial provider, arranging to use SLIP or PPP will give you the opportunity to access the Internet via the user interface on your stand-alone computer (MS Windows, Macintosh, or Xwindows), and this may be preferable to the UNIX command line interface that is common for dial-up users.

In spite of this convenience, SLIP and PPP are not for the faint of heart. Commercial access providers charge more for SLIP or PPP access, and you'll have to find and install Internet applications on your own.

The Human Touch: Networked Applications

The protocols and cabling that make up the Internet give us a network over which messages can be transmitted from one place to another. The Internet's ability to move messages around has a great deal in common with other familiar networks (the postal service, the telephone system, tin cans connected by string) whose main purpose is to allow people to communicate with each other. How people interact with each other through these other networks is perfectly clear: the letter carrier hands you a stack of mail and you read it. We all know to pick up the phone when it rings and begin talking.

On the Internet, getting people in touch with the network and each other is the job of software applications, the tools that enable us to communicate with others and to access data of all sorts throughout the Internet.

Using these tools is not particularly difficult, but their use is not yet as familiar as that of telephones or tin cans. Some of the applications you will encounter on the Internet (mail, telnet, and ftp, for example) are practically universal because they are bundled with the network portion of the UNIX operating system and are very likely to be included with networking packages for other operating systems as well.

Other Internet tools (gopher, WAIS, WWW, and archie, for example) are not part of any operating system. They were developed within the Internet community to simplify access to worldwide resources. These programs are generally not commercial software in the usual sense, but they are not hard to find on the Internet.

Later chapters will show you how to find out whether these tools are available to you, and how to use them if they are. Most of the rich diversity of applications in use on the Internet today work the same way. They share a common structure that is different from that of stand-alone applications. Understanding this structure and how it differs from that of stand-alone programs will simplify learning how things work on the Internet.

The Limits of Stand-Alone Programs

Conventional, stand-alone computer programs are able to get all resources they need from local sources, usually one or more files located on a disk on the computer where the program is run. Such programs work well in an environment where everything (the user, the computer, the program, and the data) is private and nothing needs to be shared.

However, when data needs to be shared among a group of users (or a group of computers), stand-alone programs lose some of their usefulness. Trying to use a stand-alone program to share data among several users will require one of two things: either the data must be replicated on many machines, or everyone must run the program on the one machine that holds the data. Copying the same data everywhere wastes disk space, and forcing all the interested users to run on one computer is likely to create performance problems (as well as interpersonal conflicts). Simply introducing a network in which to run stand-alone applications will not solve this problem. The underlying program architecture needs to change.

The Network Application Alternative

To overcome these limits, network applications are built on the "client/server" model. Tools based on this architecture distribute the work of one application across two programs, a client and a server, that carry on a dialog with each other over the network. Virtually all of the applications that are used to reach resources on the Internet use the client/server model. The client/server approach to networked applications is also what enables the Internet to be more than a vehicle for personal communication. Many networks provide person-to-person communication; what the Internet provides beyond this is access to information on everything from agriculture to intergalactic space science. Client/server applications make it possible for anyone with Internet access to use much of this data "anonymously," that is, without having to know someone (or to be known by someone) at the institution that publishes the data. Thanks largely to client/server architecture (and the broadmindedness of the many people who administer data sources on the Internet), your ability to access data on the Internet does not depend on who you know.

The Dialog between Clients and Servers

The basic structure of a client/server application is fairly simple. A diagram of this structure appears in Figure 1.6. When you need information or access to some resource, you start up a program (a "client") and supply the details about what you need. The client program opens a connection (usually over the network) to a server program that controls the information requested.

The dialog between client and server takes place using application protocols. The client formats your request in an application protocol it shares with the server and then dispatches the request by handing it

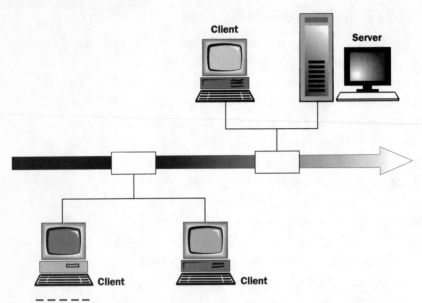

 figure 1.6 Client/Server Architecture

to one of the protocol handlers that will format the message for transmission across the network to the server.

NOTE

Here, the term server also refers to a program. In other contexts you may be familiar with, it is common to describe a computer as a server when it provides some resource (disks or file systems, printers, and so forth) for other machines on a network. Server programs can be designed to manage almost any kind of resource. We usually think first of database servers, but there are servers for other resources as well.

The server receives the client's request, evaluates it, finds the desired resource or information, formats the result in an application protocol, and passes the response to the appropriate protocol handler to begin a network transmission back to the client.

When the client receives the requested information, it provides an interface through which you can either view the information or direct it elsewhere. When you are through with the results and have no further requests, you simply exit the client program.

Client programs are always run ad hoc. You start a client when you have a question or need some information. You use the client to make specific requests and then stop the program when the needed information or resources have been provided. Server programs, on the other hand, run continuously. When there are no active clients, the server continues to run, monitoring whatever channels have been set up for clients to submit requests.

Client/server applications are extraordinarily versatile. The client and server programs can be run on the same computer or (given a sufficiently robust network) on different computers thousands of miles apart. A client/server dialog can occur between programs on computers of wildly different architectures.

Clients can be built to maintain multiple, simultaneous connections to a server or even to connect to more than one server at a time. Servers can be programmed to open connections to other servers. Clients and servers can be built to support multiple network protocols.

Interface Issues

The Internet itself does not really have a user interface. Instead, each client program provides an interface that is appropriate for the services to which it gives access. Predicting what sort of workstations will be used to run a client program is difficult, and so client programs are often distributed in different versions for different interfaces.

The ASCII version of a client has the least extravagant hardware requirements. This is particularly helpful for users who don't have access to workstations with graphical user interfaces (GUIs) or users whose only access to Internet is indirect, that is, through `telnet` or through a dial-up connection. It's important to remember that the

HOW DO CLIENTS FIND SERVERS?

By now you're probably wondering how clients connect to servers. When a server is running, it listens for client connections at a particular address that was programmed into it. On the Internet this address is called a *port number*. Port numbers are always relative to the IP address of an Internet host. To connect to a server, a client program must know which host the server is running on and what port number the server monitors for connections.

For example, the `finger` command we discussed earlier is a client/server application. When you issue a `finger` command, a connection is made to a finger server (named `fingerd`) on the computer you specify. By convention, the `finger` server monitors port 79 for connections, and this port number has been programmed into the `finger` client.

Earlier, in the sidebar on troubleshooting the `finger` command, we used `telnet` as a substitute for `finger`. That was possible because both `telnet` and `finger` use the same application protocol. `Telnet` is programmed to use port 23, but you can override this by supplying an alternate port number on the `telnet` command line. The command

```
telnet xi.uleth.ca 79
```

directs `telnet` to connect to the port monitored by the `finger` server at `xi.uleth.ca`. Once the connection is made, you must provide the name of the user you want the `finger` server to look up for you.

client program must run on a computer on the Internet in order to connect to a server. In addition to ASCII versions of client programs, there may also be versions for different GUIs (Xwindows, Macintosh, and MS-Windows versions are all popular).

Detecting and Responding to Errors

Along with the data you asked for, the client program may also deliver messages when things go wrong during the client/server dialog. The important thing to remember is that the client program is not necessarily the source of the errors it reports. It may be relaying messages originating in the server or anywhere along the path between client and server. Knowing the general structure of the client/server interaction can be helpful in figuring out what to do next. (Specific error messages are covered in Chapter 2.)

The Next Step: From Practical Perspective to Practice

You now have a high-level view of what the Internet is and a rough notion of how it works. By developing this understanding, you have already taken the first step in learning how to work with the Internet and what you can use it for. The next step is to sit down at a computer and begin using the Internet itself to build on what you already know.

Using Internet: Network Discovery Tools

Feeling a little like spies, a small group of copywriters in the advertising firm of Wittgenstein, Sellars, Quine, Putnam and Davidson (WSQP&D) huddled around a personal computer. The woman at the keyboard instructed the modem to dial the number of another computer across town. The other computer answered, and the woman typed a command. After a few seconds, she frowned at the screen. "That gopher's not answering, I'll have to try another one."

- After a few more commands had been issued, the screen filled with a menu. The woman selected an innocuous item labeled "Libraries" and another menu appeared. One entry near the bottom of the screen was titled "Reference Works," and she chose that. "When are we gonna get to the good stuff?" someone groaned. On the screen another menu appeared. "There it is," another voice said. An index finger poked at the menu item named "CIA World Factbook". Over the operator's shoulder people began calling out the names of countries to be searched.

Getting Your Bearings
without Losing Your Marbles

Now that you know roughly how the Internet works, you might well
wonder what people actually do on the Internet. What you can do
on the Internet is limited only by your knowledge and what the computer that is your point of contact with the Internet is able to do.
Throughout this book you'll develop the skills for using the Internet
effectively. In this chapter we're going to examine more closely the
computer that is your point of contact with the Internet. We'll present some tools to help you get oriented on that computer, and we'll
take a quick inventory of the Internet applications it offers.

Where You and the Internet Meet

Your point of contact with the Internet is a computer on a local network that is connected to the Internet. Having a point of contact
with the Internet allows you to work with resources all over the
world as though they were a part of your local network. In most
cases, the computer that is your entry point to the Internet will use
the Internet Protocol to communicate with the local network, and it
will have an IP address and a host name. The local network of which
your computer is a part will ordinarily be identifed to the rest of the
Internet by a domain name that can be used by people on other networks to address people and computers on your local network. Macintosh users on an AppleTalk network will encounter a slightly
different structure: the AppleTalk network must include a gateway to
a TCP/IP network that is in turn connected to the Internet.

The tools that give you a look at your connection to the Internet
are utilities packaged with the software that implements TCP/IP protocol suite. Unless otherwise noted, the tools discussed are common

to all the major UNIX vendors (AT&T, Sun, Hewlett-Packard, IBM, Silicon Graphics, Sequent, SCO and Interactive). If your Internet access is by way of a UNIX computer, these tools will be available to you. There are minor differences in implementation between vendors. In the personal computer world, where TCP/IP is an add-on product, there are more vendors (and more products), and the packaging of utilities is less uniform. The tools discussed here are safe; they pose no risk to the security of the computer on which you use them or to the security of the Internet at large.

The ping Command

The first thing to find out is whether the computer you're working on is really in contact with the Internet. Ping is just the tool to help you figure this out. The ping command queries hosts on an IP network to verify that they're up and capable of sending and receiving network packets. Ping is a standard component of UNIX TCP/IP installations. (If you're working with a UNIX system, you can see the on-line documentation for ping with the command man ping.) Ping is also widely available in commercial TCP/IP implementations for DOS and Windows systems. It is less common in Macintosh TCP/IP packages.

The ping command line can be as simple as

```
% ping optimism
optimism is alive.
```

Notice that we didn't use a Fully Qualified Domain Name. Consequently, this command will query a computer named *optimism* on our local network. The message "optimism is alive" tells us that optimism is up, that it is capable of receiving and sending packets using the Internet Protocol, and that we can establish network connections between the machine on which we ran the ping command and optimism.

To confirm that we're connected to the Internet, we can ask ping to query a computer that we know is on the Internet. In this example we'll use trs.internic.net. This is the home of the Network Information Center's registration service and it also houses a domain name database.

```
% ping rs.internic.net
rs.internic.net is alive.
```

If you can ping rs.internic.net, you're working on a computer connected to the Internet.

The output from ping may be formatted differently on some computers. For example, if you ping rs.internic.net from the Whole Earth 'Lectronic Link (the WELL), you'll get the following:

```
well: /usr/etc/ping rs.internic.net
PING rs.internic.net: 56 data bytes 1 packets      rs.in-
ternic.net is alive!
64 bytes from 198.41.0.5: icmp_seq=0. time=380. ms
----PING Statistics----
1 packets transmitted, 1 packets received, 0% packet loss
round-trip (ms) min/avg/max = 380/380/380
```

Notice that in this example ping was executed by full path name. (On the WELL, the ping command is kept in the directory /usr/etc.) The version of ping running on the WELL provides a more detailed report. In addition to the message that rs.internic.net is alive, ping reports that it sent one packet of 56 bytes, that it received a 64-byte packet in return, and that the entire transaction took 380 milliseconds. It also reports the IP address (198.41.0.5 in this case) of the host that was pinged.

✋ CAUTION

The two examples of ping that we've cited send one query and stop. Some versions of ping don't stop after one query. They continue to issue queries, once per second, until you interrupt them (usually with Ctrl-C). If your version of ping issues queries continuously, please don't let it run on needlessly. This is potentially wasteful of Internet resources.

Interpreting Exceptions

What happens if you try to ping a computer that is down or one whose network management software is not working properly? What happens when you try to ping an Intenet host from a computer not attached to the Internet?

In all these cases ping will let you know it encountered an "exception" of some kind, and even these exceptions say something about the kind of network access your computer has. Here are the exceptions you're most likely to encounter and how best to respond to them:

```
ping: Command not found
```

You should execute the command again specifying its full path name (as we did in the example above: /usr/etc/ping rs.internic.net). For hints on where to find ping and other network discovery tools, see the accompanying sidebar.

```
ping: rs.internic.net : host unknown
```

This message means that ping could not resolve the computer name you provided into an Internet address. Rs.internic.net should be accessible from any Internet host, and failing to translate the name

WHERE THE TOOLS ARE - - - - - - - - - - - - - - - -

The set of network discovery tools packaged with UNIX systems is remarkably consistent. The major UNIX vendors all provide `ping`, `hostname` and `finger`. The `whois` command (which queries the Internet's domain name database) is included in many, but not all, packages. Unfortunately the vendors don't agree about where these utilities should be installed.

`Ping` can be found in these locations:

VENDOR	DIRECTORY
HP	`/etc`
IBM RS6000	`/etc`
Sequent	`/usr/etc`
Silicon Graphics	`/usr/etc`
Sun (SunOS 4.x)	`/user/etc`
Sun (Solaris)	`/usr/sbin`

You can find `hostname` in these locations:

VENDOR	DIRECTORY
HP	`/bin`
IBM RS6000	`/usr/bin`
Sequent	`/usr/etc`
Silicon Graphics	`/usr/bsd`
Sun (SunOS 4.x)	`/bin`
Sun (Solaris)	`/bin/ucb`

into an Internet address almost certainly means that your computer is not connected to the Internet. You may still have some access to

You can find `finger` in these locations:

VENDOR	DIRECTORY
HP	/usr/bin
IBM RS6000	/usr/bin
Sequent	/usr/ucb
Silicon Graphics	/usr/bsd
Sun (SunOS 4.x)	/usr/ucb
Sun (Solaris)	/usr/bin

You can find `whois` in these locations:

VENDOR	DIRECTORY
HP	NA
IBM RS6000	/usr/bin
Sequent	N/A
Silicon Graphics	N/A
Sun (SunOS 4.x)	/usr/ucb
Sun (Solaris)	/usr/bin

If you have trouble executing one of these commands, check that the directory in which the command is installed is in the search path for your login account. (For more information about modifying the search path, see Appendix D, "Just Enough UNIX.")

Internet facilities through electronic mail, but your local network is either not connected to the Internet or does not have adequate information to reach other Internet hosts.

```
ping: no answer from rs.internic.net
```

This message means that ping received no response to its query. Usually this indicates that the computer being pinged is down. Wait a while and repeat the ping command.

The hosts file

If you have an Internet connection, it is helpful to know a few basic facts (particularly IP address and host name) about your home computer. On most Internet hosts this information is stored in a file named hosts. The hosts file is a configuration file for the TCP/IP protocol that is created when the software to manage the TCP/IP protocol is installed. Hosts is a plain text file that contains IP addresses and host names. When the Internet was small, the hostname and IP address of every computer on the Internet could be found in the hosts file, and a copy of this file was installed on every computer on the Internet. The Internet has long since outgrown the practice of distributing a file containing the names and IP addresses of all the hosts on the network, but the hosts file on each machine is still used to hold the hostname and IP address of that machine.

On UNIX systems, the hosts file is in the /etc directory. On DOS systems the location of the hosts file will vary, but you should look for it in the directory that contains the TCP/IP software. If you're working with a Macintosh, the hosts file should be in the System Folder.

On UNIX systems you can display and read the /etc/hosts text file with the command cat /etc/hosts. Cat is the UNIX command to display a file on your screen. If you're working on a DOS system, use type /etc/hosts.

Before you display the entire file, it's prudent to check its size. On UNIX systems use the ls command; DOS users can use dir. If it's relatively small, by all means proceed. This is the sequence of UNIX commands to check the size of the `hosts` file and then display it:

```
% ls -s /etc/hosts
1       /etc/hosts        /etc/hosts takes up 1 disk block, a maximum
of 1024 bytes.
% cat /etc/hosts
#
# Host Database
#
127.0.0.1       localhost
130.214.50.59 optimism loghost
```

Each line identifying a host on the network begins with an IP address and then lists the host's name and any aliases for the host. A `hosts` file could contain information about a number of different computers. By convention, the entry in `hosts` that identifies the local computer contains the word `loghost` as an alias for the local machine. The `host` file above tells us we're working on a computer named optimism whose IP address is `130.214.50.59`.

NOTE

The entry that begins with address 127.0.0.1 is a special form of IP address that can be used to test network programs on a stand-alone host. This address is a "loopback" address: packets sent here are simply routed back to the local machine and are never seen by the network at large. Lines in the hosts file beginning with a "#" are comments.

From looking at the `hosts` file you can determine that the computer you're working on is part of a network that uses the Internet Protocol, and you can figure out the computer's IP address and name. These are things you couldn't have found out from `ping`.

The UNIX hostname Command

If you can't tell from the hosts file alone what the name and IP address of the local computer are, there are other tools to help you identify the computer that provides your Internet access. On UNIX computers using the Internet Protocol, there is a separate utility to tell you the computer's host name. The command is hostname, and this is how it is used:

```
% hostname
optimism
```

Hostname should return a name that appears in the hosts file. On some Internet hosts, the hostname command will return a Fully Qualified Domain Name:

```
% hostname
shazbat.wsqpd.com
```

If you know the local computer's name, it's a simple matter to look up its IP address in the hosts file.

The hostname command is rarely included with TCP/IP software for personal computers.

The Internet Applications Toolkit

Our final piece of discovery work is to inventory the network applications that are available. If possible, we'd also like to find the CIA World Factbook. The tools we are looking for will be discussed only briefly here. Detailed discussions of the various tools will be taken up in Parts 2 and 3.

You will find two types of networked applications on Internet hosts. Some applications come bundled with the TCP/IP network software. Telnet and ftp are nearly universal regardless of operating system. In addition to `telnet` and `ftp`, UNIX systems will almost always have `mail`, `finger`, and a utility named `whois`. Mail programs are not usually included in the TCP/IP package for personal computers, and the availability of `finger` and `whois` is spotty at best. There are other applications that are developed and maintained by the Internet community (`archie`, `gopher`, `WorldWideWeb`, and many others), which must be installed voluntarily.

The easiest way to see if an application is available is to try starting it. The applications we test may not start in the way we want, but as in the case of `ping` (described above), they won't fail irrationally. If these commands fail, they will do so in predictable ways with messages we have already discussed:

- Command not found

- Host unknown

- Connection refused

- Connection timed out

Since we're browsing to see what commands are available, "Command not found" is the most ominous failure indicator. Executing any of the bundled utilities should not produce this message. The sidebar earlier in the chapter describes where these utilities are installed on several popular UNIX systems. The community-developed applications can be installed wherever the local system administrator prefers. By convention, software outside the standard UNIX distribution is usually installed in the directory `/usr/local/bin`.

If you try to execute any of the commands discussed below and get a "Command not found" message, first check that you have typed the command properly. If you've typed the command name correctly and still get a "Command not found" response, try executing the command by full pathname (for example, `/usr/ucb/telnet` or

/usr/local/bin/gopher). If executing the commands by full path-name fares no better, it is time to consult your system administrator.

Remote login using telnet

Telnet, covered in Chapter 4, is a program used to start a login session on any computer on the network. Many databases on the Internet are accessible only through telnet. For example, the agricultural database at California State University in Fresno (discussed in Chapter 1) can only be reached by a telnet request to caticsuf.csufresno.edu. The login prompt for that computer provides instructions for logging in and registering to use the database.

When you're using telnet to access some service, you will need a valid login name and password for the computer you're connecting to. All that we need to test telnet, however, is a host name. Since we know the fully qualified domain name for optimism, we can test telnet by using it to start an interactive connection from optimism to itself:

```
% telnet optimism.wsqpd.com
Trying...
Connected to optimism.wsqpd.com
Escape character is '^]'.
SunOS UNIX (optimism)
login: ^]
telnet> quit
Connection closed.
```

A telnet command consists of the word telnet and a host name (or IP address). You should see two informational messages as telnet starts. The first message reports the host that telnet will attempt to reach. Some versions of telnet will identify the host by IP address; some will identify the host by name. The second message notes what the "escape" character is. Since you're starting an interactive session with another host, most of what you type will just be passed directly to that host. Typing the escape character (in this case Control-]) will interrupt the

50

interactive session and let you give commands directly to `telnet`.

In this case the connection was made and the next line is a login prompt from optimism. Rather than log in, we typed the escape character and issued a `quit` command to close the interactive session.

Transfering Files with ftp

`Ftp`, covered in Chapter 3, is a generic file transfer program. It can be used to connect to another host specifically to move files between the two computers. Like `telnet`, `ftp` expects a host name (or IP address) on its command line and requires a valid login name and password.

```
% ftp optimism
Connected to optimism.
220 optimism FTP server (Version 2.0WU(10) Fri Apr 9 13:43:51
PDT 1993) ready. Name (optimism: bennett): bennett
331 Password required for bennett.
Password:
230 User bennett logged in.
ftp> quit
221 Goodbye.
```

`Ftp` opened the connection to the host we indicated (in this case connecting `optimism` to itself), prompted for a login name (suggesting our current login name as a default), and a password. When the login procedure succeeded, `ftp` prompted for further activity with the `ftp>` prompt. Since we're just checking that `ftp` is available, we can quit.

Internet Community Tools: archie

`Archie` is a program to help you locate files that are accessible through `ftp` on the Internet. Information about the availability of files is kept on several servers, and the `archie` program you run is a client that can query these servers with a keyword you specify.

If you just want to see whether `archie` is available on your system, type `archie` and press Return. If the `archie` client is installed, you will get a summary of the options the archie command allows. We'll discuss those in detail in Chapter 3.

Archie is one of the tools that might be of help in locating the CIA World Factbook. Since all we know about it is its name, we can try using "factbook" as a search string for archie:

```
% archie factbook
Host bric-a-brac.apple.com
     Location: /alug
               DIRECTORY drwxr-xr-x       512 May 14 1992 factbook
```

Archie has found a directory named factbook on a computer named bric-a-brac in the apple.com domain. This may not sound like much, but it's enough information to let you put ftp to use. The next step is to use ftp to connect to bric-a-brac:

```
% ftp bric-a-brac.apple.com
Connected to bric-a-brac.apple.com.
220 bric-a-brac.apple.com FTP server (IG Version 5.91 (from BU,
from UUNET 5.51
 Fri Nov 8 17:06:51 PST 1991) ready.
Name (bric-a-brac.apple.com:bennett): anonymous
331 Guest login ok, send ident as password.
Password:
230 Guest login ok, access restrictions apply.
ftp> cd alug/factbook
250 CWD command successful.
ftp> dir
200 PORT command successful.
150 Opening ASCII mode data connection for /bin/ls.
total 6088
-rw-r--r-- 1 sac archivis 1913740 Dec 22 1991 wrldfctbk
-rw-r--r-- 1 sac archivis 2140628 Jan 11 1992 wrldfctbk.91
-rw-r--r-- 1 sac archivis 880629 Jan 8 1992 wrldfctbk.91.Z
-rw-r--r-- 1 sac archivis 1275679 May 14 1992
wrldfctbk.91.stack.hqx
226 Transfer complete.
293 bytes received in     0.1 seconds (2.7 Kbytes/s)
ftp> quit
221 CUL8R.
```

As you can see, ftp manages to be verbose and cryptic at the same time. Very briefly, what happened in this session is that ftp was started with bric-a-brac's full name. After a message telling us what version of ftp we're using, ftp prompted for a login name and suggested "bennett" as a default with a reminder that the name must be valid on bric-a-brac. The login name "anonymous" was used, and ftp prompted for a password, suggesting that an identifier be used. The password bennett@optimism.wsqpd.com was typed but not echoed, and the guest login was confirmed.

From archie we have only a reference to a directory named factbook that is a subdirectory of /alug. Fortunately, we don't have to know what alug stands for to look at its contents. We issued a command to change directory (cd) to alug/factbook. When that succeeded, we asked for a listing of the contents of the directory, and found several files whose names suggest that they have something to do with the World Factbook. Interpreting file names and actually transferring files are topics that we'll cover in Chapter 3. For the time being however, we know at least one place where we can find a copy of the entire CIA World Factbook should we need it.

Internet Community Tools: gopher

The Internet gopher, covered in Chapter 6, provides menu-driven access to many of the facilities of the Internet. When you give the gopher command, you are starting a client program connected to a gopher server (by default a gopher server at the University of Minnesota, where gopher was developed). Gopher can be started by simply typing the word gopher and pressing Return. On UNIX systems this will start a "terminal-based" gopher client. Gopher is a full-screen client program, and it needs to know what kind of terminal you're using. For information on setting terminal types, see Appendix D, "Just

Enough UNIX." If a gopher client is installed on your machine and
the default server is running, you will see a menu like this:

```
% gopher
            Internet Gopher Information Client v1.11
            Root gopher server: gopher2.tc.umn.edu
  -->       1.  Information About Gopher/
            2.  Computer Information/
            3.  Discussion Groups/
            4.  Fun & Games/
            5.  Internet file server (ftp) sites/
            6.  Libraries/
            7.  News/
            8.  Other Gopher and Information Servers/
            9.  Phone Books/
           10.  Search Gopher Titles at the University of Minne-
sota <?>
           11.  Search lots of places at the University of Minne-
sota <?>
           12.  University of Minnesota Campus Information/
Press ? for Help, q to Quit, u to go up a menu
Page: 1/1
```

Gopher clients have good error-handling facilities and will generally tell you if something goes wrong in the connection procedure.

If you feel that a gopher client has paused for an unreasonable time
waiting to connect to a server, you can abort the gopher client by typing Ctrl-C (^C).

At the beginning of this chapter, the staff at WSQP&D found the
CIA World Factbook through gopher. Gopher offers a slightly different perspective on this resource from that offered by ftp. From the
menu above, select item 6, Libraries. That selection produces a menu
of things related to libraries, and one item on that menu is Reference
Works. This selection bring up a menu with an entry for the CIA
World Factbook. That item in turn displays a menu with entries
describing the Factbook and its contents and a series of items for the
letters of the alphabet. Selecting a letter will bring up a menu of
Factbook articles for countries beginning with that letter. Simply

select the country name from this menu to view its article.

Internet Community Tools: WWW

The WorldWide Web, covered in Chapter 7, provides a hypertext interface to many things on the Internet. *Hypertext* is a system for cross-referencing and retrieving related documents. Using a special viewer (called a "browser") you can read a hypertext document as you would any other. However, the browser will also highlight any elements of the current document that are cross-referenced to other documents. When you select a cross reference, the browser will retrieve the referenced document for you to read (and that, of course, may lead to other documents in turn).

www is a hypertext browser. It is a screen-oriented tool (like gopher) that provides an orderly set of choices for navigating through Internet resources.

You start the WorldWideWeb application by typing www and pressing Return. Normally this will present a hypertext "home page" on your screen.

As with gopher, testing the www client program requires connecting to a www server. If this connection fails or appears to hang, type Ctrl-C to abort the session.

The Next Fifteen Minutes

These exercises have given you the tools to find a great deal of useful information about your point of contact with the Internet and the available applications for reaching resources over the network. In Part II we will begin to use the essential network application tools in earnest: ftp, telnet, and mail.

First

Generation

Internet

Applications:

FTP,

Telnet,

and

E-Mail

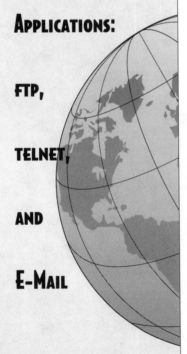

There are three fundamental application services on the Internet: file transfer, remote login, and electronic mail. Standard versions of `ftp` (the Internet's file transfer program) and `telnet` (the Internet's remote login program) are virtually universal among computers on the Internet.

- In Chapter 3 you'll learn how to use `ftp` and `archie` to find files and move them between Internet hosts. The technique of "anonymous" `ftp` allows anyone on the Internet to copy files from sites with public archives. `Archie` is a database of files accessible through anonymous `ftp`.

- `Telnet` is discussed in Chapter 4. Remote login is the feature of the Internet that brings Bulletin Board Services and Library Card Catalogs within any user's reach.

- Electronic mail offers an unparalleled ability to interact with people and information resources. In Chapter 5, you'll discover the basics of sending and receiving e-mail and some tips on using mail to reach resources across network boundaries.

CHAPTER

Using ftp, the Internet File Transfer Program

He arrived at work Monday morning to find a yellow PostIt stuck in the center of his computer's screen. It so offended his sense of tidiness that he almost threw it away unread. But the message was short enough to be read in one glance and cryptic enough to overcome his irritation. It read simply

```
finger yanoff@csd4.csd.uwm.edu
and follow instructions for ftp!
```

- Finger, he knew, was a UNIX command. He recognized that yanoff was a user name, evidently a user on a computer named csd4 in domains named csd (computer science department, perhaps?), uwm (probably a university somewhere), and edu (uwm was definitely an educational institution of some kind). He was not at all sure about ftp (it made him think of Bill the Cat), but with the command `man ftp` he soon discovered that it was a program for transferring files over the Internet.

- He logged in and executed the command from the yellow note. His screen filled with information about something called the Internet Services List and its author Scott Yanoff. Also on his screen were instructions for using ftp to retrieve a copy of the Internet Services List.

- He had never used ftp before, but it didn't seem all that complicated, so he gave it a try. A few minutes later he had copied Yanoff's list to his own computer. Skimming through it he realized that the Internet Services List was a quick reference card for all sorts of services available on the Internet: it contained brief instructions for accessing dozens of bulletin boards and databases. It listed sites with files available for copying with ftp. It described archie servers and where to get up-to-the-minute baseball scores and stock quotes. He resolved to think more charitably of the colleague who had left the PostIt on his screen and to learn more about the ftp command.

Information To Go

The Internet is a great deal more than a global reference library. One of its distinguishing features is that many of the resources on the network are available for you to copy onto your computer free of charge. Files containing information, source code, and even compiled programs are stored in publicly accessible directories. The contents of these directories are then published in one way or another and anyone with network access can copy the files for their own use. A quick look through Yanoff's List of Internet Services shows at least forty sites from which files can be copied.

Copying files quickly and accurately from computer to computer over the Internet is a technological achievement that we often take for granted. If you think about it, the odds against successful file transfers are impressive. To begin with, a file can contain just about anything: plain text, source code for some program, data in goodness knows what format, or binary stuff to be executed by some chip somewhere. Clearly not all files are the same. Add to that the complexity of copying files between computers that have different operating systems, different processors, and even different ways of sequencing bytes, and the task of transferring files accurately seems even more daunting. Nevertheless, ftp provides just such a service, transferring any sort of file between any pair of computers on the Internet. In the following pages we'll discuss

- Getting ready to use ftp

- How anonymous ftp works

- Basic ftp commands

- Using archie to find files available for ftp.

Getting Ready to Use ftp

The hardest part of using ftp may be collecting the information needed to locate the file to be transferred. As in the case of Yanoff's list and the CIA World Factbook mentioned in Chapter 2, you need to know the name of the machine to which ftp should connect and the full pathname of the file you're interested in.

The Internet offers many ways to locate files you might be interested in downloading:

- The list of Internet Services is one tool for locating files to transfer.

- The USENET newsgroups (discussed more fully in Chapter 8) are another helpful source of information concerning publicly available files.

- In Chapter 2 we introduced archie as a tool to perform keyword searches of ftp archives. Later in this chapter, we'll work with archie in greater detail.

Besides the name and location of the file you want to copy, you should also be aware of both the type and the size of files you intend to transfer. For example, you probably don't want to copy Macintosh program files to an IBM PC. And if you have only 1 MB of disk storage space available, you won't be able to download a file as large as the complete CIA World Factbook. You can use ftp's dir command to check file sizes, but determining file types is largely a matter of knowing how to interpret file names.

A File Name Primer

In the ftp archives on the Internet, you will encounter files for all sorts of computers. Some of these files will be plain text, some will be binary. Many will be compressed to conserve space at the site that has published the file. If you know the most common file naming conventions, you will be able to find the files you want more quickly.

Table 3.1 lists the naming conventions you are most likely to run into on the Internet. Extensions are divided into ASCII (or text) and binary, the two file types that matter most to ftp.

table 3.1: Common ASCII and Binary File Name Extensions

CATEGORY	EXTENSION	MEANING
ASCII	.c	C Programming Language Source Code
	.h	C Programming Language Header File
	.txt	Text (ASCII) file
	.uu	ASCII file produced by uuencode
	.bat	DOS Batch file
	.shar	UNIX Shell Archive
	.ps	PostScript file
	.hqx	Macintosh BinHexed file release 4.0 or earlier.
Binary	.EXE	Executable binary file (DOS or VAX/VMS)
	.COM	Executable binary file (DOS)
	.Z	Binary file created by compress
	.sit	StuffIt file for Macintosh
	.gz	file compressed with GNU gzip
	.hqx	Macintosh BinHexed file release 5.0 or greater.

Classifying files according to these conventions can sometimes be problematic. For example, the BinHex format used on Macintosh changed from ASCII to binary between release 4 and release 5. Similarly, the .COM extension designates a binary file under MS-DOS and an ASCII file under VAX/VMS.

In the personal computer world there has been a proliferation of programs to archive and compress groups of files. Downloading a compressed file requires that you have the correct software to decompress it on the target computer. Fortunately, a comprehensive table summarizing file compression software and naming conventions by platform is available via anonymous `ftp` in the file `/doc/pcnet/compression` at `ftp.cso.uiuc.edu`. This file is updated periodically as new tools for file compression become available. By getting this information from the Internet itself, you can be sure that you're getting the most up-to-date information available.

Using ftp

`Ftp` establishes a connection between two computers for the purpose of exchanging files. When you use `ftp`, the Internet host from which you issue the `ftp` command is the "local" computer. Your `ftp` command starts a client program that connects to an `ftp` server (also called an `ftp` "daemon") on the "remote" computer. You must identify the remote computer by name or IP address on the `ftp` command line:

```
% ftp name.domain.qualified.fully
```

You can use `ftp` to make a connection to any computer on the Internet on which you have an account. The login name and password you provide must be valid on the remote computer. The login information that you use on your local computer will not automatically be usable on the remote system.

Most Internet users do not have accounts on all the machines from which they want to copy files. (And no administrator of an Internet host wants to be bogged down adding individual accounts for all the users throughout the network who might want to exchange files with that host.) Therefore, the Internet sites that publish files to be copied via ftp usually offer a special login name (anonymous) that anyone on the Internet can use to log in via ftp. When you log in as anonymous, the remote system may prompt you with instructions for what to enter in place of a password. Frequently, you will be asked to supply something (for example, your electronic mail address) that identifies who you are and how you can be reached. The sample session for downloading Yanoff's list of Internet resources, in the accompanying sidebar, illustrates this prompting.

GETTING YANOFF'S LIST – – – – – – – – – – – – – – – – –

Scott Yanoff's instructions for getting the Internet Services List via ftp are terse, but they tell you everything you need to know:

ftp csd4.csd.uwm.edu (available in pub/inet.services.txt).

By now you probably recognize csd4.csd.uwm.edu as a fully qualified domain name. The file you want to transfer is named inet.services.txt, and it is located in a directory named pub. The .txt suffix indicates that the file is a text or ASCII file. The only additional piece of information you might want is the login name and password to use when ftp prompts you for these things. As a general rule, use anonymous to log in to machines on which you have no personal account. Ftp will tell you if a password is required, and often you will be asked to enter your electronic mail address (for example, bennett@wsqpd.com) as the password. By default ftp provides status messages about every command you execute. You'll see a three-digit number preceding each message. You can suppress these messages with the **verbose** command. An ftp session to download the list to your computer should look something like this:

```
% ftp csd4.csd.uwm.edu    Fully Qualified Domain Name of remote
computer
Connected to csd4.csd.uwm.edu.
220 csd4.csd.uwm.edu FTP server (ULTRIX Version 4.1 Tue Mar 19
00:38:17 EST 1991) ready.
Name (csd4.csd.uwm.edu:bkf): anonymous    Log in as "anonymous"
331 Guest login ok, send ident as password.
Password:   Use your E-mail address as password; it won't be echoed
on the screen.
230 Guest login ok, access restrictions apply.
ftp> cd pub    Change to pub directory
250 CWD command successful.
ftp> dir i*    List files in pub whose names start with "i"
200 PORT command successful
150 Opening data connection for /bin/ls (192.100.81.108,3787) (0
bytes).
-rwxr-xr-x  1 5304    -2        362740 Jun 15  1992 icb
-rw-r--r--  1 4494    -2         29474 Jul  1 12:46 inet.serv-
ices.txt
-rw-r--r--  1 4494    -2         21968 Jul  2 10:54 internetwork-
mail-guide
226 Transfer complete.
remote: i*
211 bytes received in 0.02 seconds (10 Kbytes/s)
ftp> get inet.services.txt    Fetch the file "inet.services.txt"
200 PORT command successful.
150 Opening data connection for inet.services.txt
(192.100.81.108,3789) (29474 bytes).
226 Transfer complete.
local: inet.services.txt remote: inet.services.txt
30043 bytes received in 0.85 seconds (35 Kbytes/s)
ftp> quit    Close the FTP session
221 Goodbye.
```

Connecting to another computer via ftp is very much like logging in to the remote computer. If you use a regular login account to make the connection, your ftp session will start from that account's home directory, and you can work directly with the files there or move to another directory. When you connect to another system anonymously, ftp also gives you a working directory. The initial directory for anonymous ftp sessions is the root directory of a special tree of directories that has been set up both to ensure the security of the remote system and to make it easy for you to move from directory to directory and find the files you want to copy.

Once you've connected to a remote system, you will receive an ftp> prompt. From this prompt you can issue simple commands (get and put, discussed below) to move files between the two computers. Again, the sidebar on Yanoff's list illustrates this process.

Taming ftp

Ftp is not the world's friendliest program, but it's far from hostile. You can use ftp perfectly well knowing only five commands: ascii, binary, get, put, and quit. However, using get and put is much simpler if you first take a few minutes to set up some things about your ftp session and move to the directory that contains the files you want to transfer. The most important commands to control an ftp session are:

ascii	Assume transferred files are text (default).
binary	Assume transferred files are binary (image).
cr	Toggle stripping of carriage returns from ASCII files.
hash	Print hash marks to controlling terminal during transfers.

prompt	Toggle prompting on or off during multiple file transfers.
status	Display current status of all settable options.
user	Set login name and password.
verbose	Toggle verbose messages on/off.

The single most important decision you will need to make in working with ftp concerns the type of file transfer you want ftp to make: ascii or binary. This choice will determine whether the files

GETTING HELP WITH FTP — — — — — — — — — —

You should be aware that ftp has a built-in help facility that can be invoked with by typing help or ? in response to the ftp> prompt. The default help is a list of all the available commands:

```
ftp> help
Commands may be abbreviated. Commands are:
!          cr         ls         prompt     runique
$          delete     macdef     proxy      send
account    debug      mdelete    sendport   status
append     dir        mdir       put        struct
ascii      disconnect mget       pwd        sunique
bell       form       mkdir      quit       tenex
binary     get        mls        quote      trace
bye        glob       mode       recv       type
case       hash       mput       remotehelp user
cd         help       nmap       rename     verbose
cdup       image      ntrans     reset      ?
close      lcd        open       rmdir
```

All of these commands are discussed in the the on-line documentation for ftp. On UNIX systems, you can display this information at any time by typing man ftp.

you retrieve with ftp are usable or not, and unfortunately, there is no universally correct choice. (Table 3.1, earlier in this chapter, lists common ASCII and binary filename extensions.) The default transfer type is ascii, but it is always a good idea to check this setting (with the status command) before transferring files.

With the file type set to ascii, ftp will make adjustments to the file being transferred to compensate for differences between the local and remote machines that affect the readability of text files. Thus, for ascii transfers, ftp will adjust the end-of-line sequence to whatever is conventional for the receiving machine. When the file type is set to binary, ftp produces an exact byte-for-byte image of any file it must copy.

TIP

Choosing ascii or binary depends on both the file's contents and on how you intend to use it. There are two rules of thumb that will be helpful in making this choice. (1) If the file you're going to download will ultimately be used on another computer with a different architecture or operating system, use binary representation for the download. (2) If you expect to read the file with the local machine's generic program for displaying files (such as the DOS type command or the UNIX cat command), use the ASCII type of transfer. If you don't expect to view the file on the local machine, you should probably choose binary representation for your file transfer.

The cr command controls how ftp handles the carriage return characters that occur as part of the end-of-line sequence in ASCII files on some computers. On UNIX systems, the end-of-line is marked by a linefeed character. On many other systems (DOS, for example) the end-of-line sequence is carriage-return/linefeed. When cr is turned on (the default setting), ftp will strip carriage returns from text files. To preserve carriage returns, toggle cr off.

Ftp is usually silent during file transfers. Most ftp transfers are completed in a matter of seconds, but if very large files are being moved or if the network is sluggish, a transfer can take several minutes. The hash command provides a way to monitor ftp's progress during a file transfer. When hash is toggled on, a "hash mark" (#) is printed to your screen for each block of data transferred.

The hash command has another important use. Some systems on the Internet automatically disconnect users who are inactive for some period of time. During a long file transfer, when you aren't typing on the keyboard, your login session on the local machine may appear to be idle. Setting hash on sends a steady stream of characters to your screen during the file transfer, and this will signal the system that your login session is still active.

The prompt command controls how ftp behaves during transfers of groups of files. By default prompting is on, and you will be asked to confirm each file transfer. If you want to transfer multiple files without interruption, use the prompt command to toggle prompting off.

The status command displays the current setting of all ftp's optional features. Use this command if you're unsure about which options are currently enabled. A typical status report looks like this:

```
ftp> status
Not connected.
No proxy connection.
Mode: stream; Type: ascii; Form: non-print; Structure: file
Verbose: on; Bell: off; Prompting: on; Globbing: on Store
unique: off; Receive unique: off
Case: off; CR stripping: on
Ntrans: off
Nmap: off
Hash mark printing: off; Use of PORT cmds: on
```

The user command allows you to specify the user name and password that ftp will use in making a connection to a remote computer. It lets you recover from failed logins when you first start ftp.

By default ftp is very verbose: all the responses from the ftp server are printed on your screen during an ftp session. (These messages are also illustrated in the Yanoff sample session.) The verbose command lets you suppress these messages when you want.

Working with Directories

Whenever you connect to a remote computer with ftp, the ftp server on that computer will assign a current or working directory to your session. If you have logged in as a regular user, the working directory

FAQs, FTP, AND YOU

Many systems on the Internet collect Frequently Asked Questions (and their answers). FAQs have become an Internet institution, and often this supplemental documentation is more helpful than the official manual because it addresses questions that have come up in the course of actually using the Internet.

There is no standard way to access FAQs. Some systems have a special utility that can be used to query specific topics or keywords. Other systems keep their FAQs in files that anyone can browse.

Even if your local Internet system doesn't maintain FAQs, you may still be able to get FAQs from other sources. For example, much of the Internet lore regarding ftp originates in the USENET newsgroups where ftp is a frequent topic of discussion, and FAQs about ftp can be found as a regular part of the archives for these newsgroups. USENET is the subject of Chapter 8. Later in this chapter, we'll use archie to locate these FAQs.

will be the login directory for that user. If you have logged in anonymously, the working directory will be the root directory of a special directory tree reserved exclusively for anonymous ftp. In either case, ftp provides some commands for moving around among the directories on the remote machine. These commands are similar to the directory navigation commands for UNIX. Examples of these commands in use appear in Listing 3.1.

pwd	Print working (current) directory for remote system.
cd	Change directory on remote system (requires directory name).
cdup	Change directory on remote system to the parent of the current directory.
dir	List the contents of a directory on the remote system including name, permissions, owner, and size.
mdir	List the contents of the multiple directories on the remote system including name, permissions, owner, and size.
ls	List the contents of a directory on the remote system by name only.
mls	List the contents of multiple directories on the remote system by name only.
lcd	Change the working directory on the local system (requires directory name).

listing 3.1:
Examples of FTP Directory Navigation

```
ftp> pwd    Print the name of the current directory.
257 "/" is current directory.
ftp> dir    List contents of current directory.
200 PORT command successful.
150 Opening data connection for /bin/ls  (0 bytes).
total 7
-rw-r--r--  1 0        0              1592 Mar 23  1992 Policy
dr-xr-xr-x  2 0        0               512 Oct 24  1991 bin
dr-xr-xr-x  2 0        0               512 May 13  1992 etc
d-wxr-xr-x  2 480      -2              512 Jun 29 13:04 incoming
dr-xrwxrwt 35 480      -2             1536 Jul  1 18:29 pub
226 Transfer complete.
375 bytes received in 0.25 seconds (1.5 Kbytes/s)
ftp> dir pub/i*   List names of files in pub dir beginning with "i".
200 PORT command successful.
150 Opening data connection for /bin/ls  (0 bytes).
-rwxr-xr-x  1 5304     -2           362740 Jun 15  1992 pub/icb
-rw-r--r--  1 4494     -2            29474 Jul  1 12:46
pub/inet.services.txt
-rw-r--r--  1 4494     -2            21968 Jul  2 10:54
pub/internetwork-mail-guide
226 Transfer complete.
remote: pub/i*
223 bytes received in 0.074 seconds (2.9 Kbytes/s)

ftp> cd     cd command with no target
(remote-directory) pub    ftp prompts for target
250 CWD command successful.
ftp> ls i*    list files beginning with "i" again.
200 PORT command successful.
150 Opening data connection for /bin/ls  (0 bytes).
icb
inet.services.txt
internetwork-mail-guide
226 Transfer complete.
remote: i*
49 bytes received in 0.0045 seconds (11 Kbytes/s)

ftp> cdup    change to parent directory
250 CWD command successful.
```

```
ftp> ls    list contents of new working directory
200 PORT command successful.
150 Opening data connection for /bin/ls  (0 bytes).
Policy
bin
etc
incoming
pub
226 Transfer complete.
42 bytes received in 0.087 seconds (0.47 Kbytes/s)
ftp> quit
221 Goodbye.
```

Pwd and cdup are relatively simple to use. Neither command requires you to provide any further information. You simply type pwd, and ftp reports the current directory on the remote system. Similarly, when you type cdup, ftp moves you to the parent of the current directory and makes that the new working directory.

The cd command must be given the name of a directory on the remote machine. If this name is omitted, ftp will prompt for a directory name.

The dir and ls commands differ only in the amount of information they show about a directory. Dir produces the long form of the listing, and ls lists names only. If you just type dir or ls, you'll get a listing of the current directory on the remote machine.

If you want a listing of some directory other than the current one, you can include its name on the command line. To restrict the listing only to certain files, you can include a suitably wildcarded filename to indicate those files.

✗ TIP _ _ _ _ _

Directory listings can be long. If you get a listing that is longer than you expected, use Control-C (^C) to abort the listing.

Ftp uses a special pair of commands (`mdir` and `mls`) to list the contents of multiple directories. Both `mdir` and `mls` expect two command-line arguments: the remote directory to be listed, and the name of a local file in which to store the command's output. (Ftp expects this output to be so long that you won't want to browse through it on the screen.)

TIP

The `ftp` commands `mls`, `mdir`, and `get` (described below) expect the name of a local file to hold the command's output. There are occasions when you will want to review the output of your commands on the screen rather than have the output stored in a file. There are two ways to redirect output of `ftp` commands directly to the screen: (1) When prompted for a local file name, enter a hyphen (—). This will send the `ftp` output to the screen in an uninterrupted stream. (2) To control the flow of output from `ftp` with one of the UNIX commands for viewing a file one page at a time (`pg` or `more`, for example), enter ¦ `more` or ¦ `pg` (depending on which pager is available) when prompted for a local file name. This will redirect the `ftp` output to the command you specify.

Copying Files

Once you have set up your `ftp` session and maneuvered to the appropriate directory, you will need relatively few commands to do the work of moving files back and forth across the Internet:

get	Move a file from remote to local.
recv	Synonym for `get`.
put	Move a file from local to remote.
send	Synonym for `put`.

| mget | Move several files from remote to local. |
| mput | Move several files from local to remote. |

Because we're interested chiefly in anonymous ftp, we'll concentrate on the commands for downloading files (get, mget, and recv). Get copies files from the remote computer to the local one. Send does exactly the same thing in the opposite direction: it copies files from local to remote. Sending files to other sites via anonymous ftp requires a directory on the remote computer in which the anonymous user has permission to store files. Many anonymous ftp sites do not allow files to be uploaded anonymously. If you want to send a file to a site via anonymous ftp, you should first check with the administrator of the receiving site to find out what the local conventions are for uploading files.

The get Command

The get command must always include the name of the file to be copied (the source file) and may include a name for the destination file. The simplest form of the get command looks like this:

```
ftp> get inet.services.txt
200 PORT command successful.
150 Opening data connection for inet.services.txt (29474 bytes).
226 Transfer complete.
local: inet.services.txt remote: inet.services.txt 30043 bytes
received in 0.85 seconds (35 Kbytes/s)
```

This command copied the file named inet.services.txt from the remote computer to the local computer. After a get command, ftp reports the number of bytes transferred and the elapsed time for the transfer.

This simple version of the get command depends on a series of assumptions. It assumes that the file to be copied is in the current directory on the remote machine, that the local machine's copy should also be named inet.services.txt, and that the local copy should be created in the current directory for the ftp session on the local machine. You must have permission to create files in the current directory of the local computer for this command to succeed. If you don't have such permission, you'll get a "permission denied" message like the following:

```
ftp> get inet.services.txt
inet.services.txt: Permission denied
```

If you want to specify either the source or destination files by pathname, you can do so, but it takes a little extra care. The general syntax is this:

```
get source destination
```

where *source* and *destination* each specify a pathname. For example, the following command gets a remote file named faq from a directory named pub/ftp-list and creates a local copy of it called ftp.faq in the /tmp directory of the local machine:

```
get pub/ftp-lis/faq /tmp/ftp.faq
```

The destination filename must be a complete path that includes the file name. If you provide a destination name that consists only of a directory path (/tmp, for example), ftp will tell you that /tmp is a directory and not legal as a name for the destination file.

TIP

On UNIX systems, /tmp is a directory in which any user can create files. If you have problems with directory permissions and ftp, you can place destination files in /tmp. Remember to include both the path and the file name (/tmp/filename) when specifying the destination file. As its name implies, /tmp is used for temporary storage. Many UNIX applications put their temporary files in this directory. It is not a good practice to put large files in /tmp, and because /tmp is periodically purged, you shouldn't use it for permanent storage. However, it is a handy directory into which you can copy small files to be moved to other directories later. If you copy files into /tmp, don't forget to delete them or move them to your own directory as soon as possible.

When your get command does not include a destination name, ftp assumes that you want the destination file to have exactly the same name as the source file, including any directories you listed as part of the source file name. However, get doesn't create directories as part of copying files. If you omitted the destination file name and included directories in the source file name (pub/ftp-list/faq, for example), those directories will have to exist at the destination site for the get command to succeed. The following example shows what happens when a get command fails because the pathname it needs at the destination site doesn't exist.

```
ftp> get pub/ftp-list/faq
pub/ftp-list/faq: no such file or directory
```

Using mget to Work with Groups of Files

The get command works with individual files only. To transfer multiple files with a single command, use mget. The mget command allows you to specify several source files on a single command line. If, for example, you wanted to copy all the files in the current directory whose names end in .c or .h, you could do so with the command

```
mget README Makefile *.c *.h
```

This command will copy all the files ending in .c or .h and the files named README and Makefile from the current directory on the remote machine. (The asterisk is a wildcard character that matches any string of characters in the file name. Thus, *.c matches all the filenames ending in .c)

Note that mget accepts only the names of files to be copied: you can't specify a target file name with mget. (Among other things, this means that the trick of using a hyphen to send a file to the screen can't be used with mget.) As with the get command, any directories

---

MLS—TESTING WILDCARD FILE SPECIFICATIONS – – – – – – – –

When you use wildcard characters like * and ? with mget, it is always a good idea to check that the wildcards will match the filenames you're interested in. Use the mls command to do this:

```
ftp> mls *.c
```

Mls simply lists the filenames that match, so you can adjust any wildcard specifications that don't find the files you want without first transferring either too many or too few files. Mls will expand only one wildcard at a time, so a command like the following will fail:

```
ftp> mls *.c *.h
```

in the source file name must already exist at the destination site for the transfer to succeed.

Beyond Yanoff: Using archie

The Internet Services List that we retrieved earlier in this chapter will provide a starting point for anyone browsing the Internet for resources of almost any sort. Along with many other things, it offers signposts to a few Internet sites that have extensive archives of files that can be retrieved through anonymous ftp. It's relatively easy to connect to one of these sites and meander among the directories looking for files of interest. But this sort of browsing is time-consuming, and if you depend on chance encounters to find interesting files, you won't have many opportunities to use ftp.

Fortunately there's a tool that will let you perform keyword searches on a database of files available on the Internet through anonymous ftp. The tool is called archie.

Archie is a project of the McGill University School of Computer Science. The heart of archie is a database containing directory listings of what is available through anonymous ftp at sereval hundred Internet sites. The database is compiled by a program that over the course of a month or so makes an ftp connection to each site and produces a listing of what the site has to offer. This database is then published to various archie servers and made available for anyone to query. The following servers host the archie database:

archie.ans.net	(USA [NY])
archie.rutgers.edu	(USA [NJ])
archie.sura.net	(USA [MD])

archie.unl.edu	(USA [NE])
archie.mcgill.ca	(Canada)
archie.funet.fi	(Finland/Mainland Europe)
archie.au	(Australia)
archie.doc.ic.ac.uk	(Great Britain/Ireland)
archie.wide.ad.jp	(Japan)
archie.ncu.edu.tw	(Taiwan)
archie.cs.huji.ac.il	(Israel)
archie.sogang.ac.kr	(Korea)
archie.nz	(New Zealand)
archie.kuis.kyoto-u.ac.jp	(Japan)
archie.th-darmstadt.de	(Germany)
archie.luth.se	(Sweden)

There are several ways to query these servers. The archie service has become so popular that the preferred ways of submitting archie queries are through an archie client program or, if your site does not have an archie client, via electronic mail. To tell whether your machine has this client, just type archie at the UNIX prompt. If you do have it, the prompt will change to archie>. If not, you'll get a message to that effect.

In Chapter 2, we used the archie client to locate the CIA World Factbook with the command:

```
%    archie factbook
```

This command found a directory named factbook that contained several different versions of the file we were looking for. When archie is given a keyword like factbook, it queries the database for the names of files or directories that contain that keyword. Many of the ftp archives on the Internet are duplicated at numerous sites, and it's important to choose keywords carefully to get results that are manageable. Archie has several options that make its keyword querying more flexible:

-c   Case-sensitive search for names containing the keyword.

-s   Case-insensitive search for names containing the keyword.

-ofile   Put the results of the search in the named file.

-m#   Limit the search to no more than # results (the default is 95).

-hserver   Query the archie database at the named *server*.

Earlier it was mentioned that FAQs often originate from USENET newsgroups. An archie query to find FAQs about ftp could take the form:

```
%     archie ftp-list
Host procyon.cis.ksu.edu
            Location: /pub/mirrors/news.answers
        DIRECTORY drwxr-xr-x      512 May 3 11:04 ftp-list
<Listing truncated.>
```

Responses to archie queries are sorted first by host name, then by location or path. After the location, archie provides a listing that shows the permissions, size, date and name of each query "hit" (match). In this case archie found many more hits than we have room to illustrate here.

Notice that we queried for ftp-list. We chose this keyword because many of the USENET newsgroups maintain their archives in the form of a mailing list to which users can subscribe. (Mailing lists will be discussed in Chapter 5). A query for ftp-list is much more specific than a query for simply ftp or faq.

Even if the archie client program is not installed on the system that provides your Internet access, you can still submit archie queries via electronic mail. For information on the mail interface to archie, pick the archie server nearest you from the list presented earlier and send a message to archie at that site. For example, there's an archie server at the University of Nebraska at Lincoln. To reach it by mail, use this command:

```
% mail archie@archie.unl.edu
Subject: ...
help
```

The user name archie in this mail address is an automated mailbox, not a human user. Archie is also the host name in this case, and that host is in the unl and edu domains. The body of your message should contain the word help. You'll get back a short user guide for the e-mail interface to archie.

HUNTING THROUGH THE INTERNET - - - - - - - - - - - - -

The *Internet Hunt* is a scavenger hunt for information from Internet sources hosted by Rick Gates. Each month 10 new questions appear, and anyone who wants to play downloads the questions and sets off to find the answers using only Internet resources. Points are awarded not just for getting the correct answer, but for doing so in a way that is intuitively satisfying, easy to figure out, and instructive about the Internet. Throughout the rest of this book, we'll have a Hunt of our own with questions (and answers) to get more familiar with the Internet and its resources.

Question 1   We mentioned in Chapter 1 how to use gopher to get information about the Internet Hunt. We won't learn about gopher in detail until Chapter 6. How would you find the real Internet Hunt if you couldn't use gopher?

Answer   An archie query will help you locate information about the Hunt if you can come up with a keyword or file name that identifies the Internet Hunt uniquely. Both hunt and internet would match file names for many, many archives. Try putting both words together. These days it is fashionable to add a placeholder character to separate words in a filename. Common placeholders are the dash (-), dot (.), and underscore (_). Using internet-hunt found what we wanted right away:

```
% archie -s internet-hunt

Host nic.cic.net

    Location: /pub
    FILE lrwxrwxrwx      21  Feb  4 17:33  internet-hunt
```

The next step is to connect to nic.cic.net with ftp and look at what's there to be sure we're on the right track:

```
% ftp nic.cic.net
Connected to nic.cic.net.
220 nic.cic.net FTP server (Version 5.60+UA) ready.
Name (nic.cic.net:bennett): anonymous
331 Guest login ok, send ident as password.
Password:
230- Guest login ok, access restrictions apply.
230 Local time is Mon Aug  9 11:18:02 1993
ftp> cd pub
ftp> dir internet-hunt
lrwxrwxrwx  1 0         1                  21 Jun 14 12:19 internet-hunt
-> ./nircomm/gopher/hunt

ftp> cd internet-hunt
ftp> dir
```

```
total 7
-rwxr-xr-x  1 0         0               207 Aug  9 15:12 .cache
-rwxr-xr-x  1 0         0               310 May 31 01:12 .cache.html
drwxr-xr-x  2 1002     20               512 Feb 19 18:14 .cap
drwxr-xr-x  3 1002     20               512 Jul 13 17:56 about
drwxr-xr-x  3 1002     20               512 May  7 15:56 comments
drwxr-xr-x  3 1002     20               512 Jul 31 08:04 questions
drwxr-xr-x  5 1002     20               512 Jul 11 21:00 results
ftp> cd about
ftp> dir
total 22
-rwxr-xr-x  1 0         0               594 Aug  9 15:12 .cache
-rwxr-xr-x  1 0         0               785 May 24 20:12 .cache.html
drwxr-xr-x  2 1002     20               512 Feb  8  1993 .cap
-rw-r--r--  1 1002     20              2472 Feb 21 16:05 00readme.txt
-rw-r--r--  1 1002     20         2458 May  8 19:22 distrib.txt
-rw-r--r--  1 1002     20         2762 Feb  8  1993 history.txt
-rw-r--r--  1 1002     20         1442 Jul 13 17:53 individ.txt
-rw-r--r--  1 1002     20         2649 May  5 20:52 intro.txt
-rw-r--r--  1 1002     20         1345 Feb  8  1993 rules.txt
-rw-r--r--  1 1002     20         1313 Feb  8  1993 scoring.txt
-rw-r--r--  1 1002     20          943 Jul 13 17:54 team.txt
ftp> get intro.txt
local: intro.txt remote: intro.txt
ftp> quit
%
```

Reading the `intro.txt` file will lead you to other files in this directory. The file `distrib.txt` describes the usual channels for distributing the Internet Hunt.

Question 2   You're about to take a trip to Sydney, Australia. Naturally you're taking your Powerbook, but you're worried about its battery. If you have to buy a replacement in Sydney, what will replacement batteries cost?

Answer   This is a little trickier than the first question. A first attempt using `whois` to locate Internet sites in Sydney or Australia turned up only the fact that the top-level domain for Australia is au. Looking through the Internet Services List for services in Australia produced an entry for databases that can be queried with the finger command at dir.su.oz.au. Accessing that service looks like this:

```
% finger help@dir.su.oz.au
[extra.ucc.su.OZ.AU]
****This is an experimental service offered free of charge by****
**** The University Computing Service, University of Sydney.****
**** Please mail support@is.su.edu.au if you have any queries.****

Finger offers these additional services:

- Access to a database facility
    Usage: finger <key>%<database>@dir.su.edu.au

    <key> is usually an "egrep" regular expression
and <database> can be:

    aarnet          - resources available on AARNet
    buildings       - buildings and their codes at Sydney Uni
    archie          - query anonymous FTP databases
    internet        - resources available on the Internet
    library         - library access available via AARNet
    newsgroups      - find NetNews newsgroups
    phone           - The Sydney Uni Phone Book
    postcodes       - Australian Postcodes
    shop            - prices at the UCS shop

-    Usage:
     finger help@dir.su.edu.au      - this help
     finger help%<database>@dir.su.edu.au
```

Now you can query for help with the price list at the UCS shop:

```
% finger help%shop@dir.su.edu.au
[extra.ucc.su.oz.au]
Help: finger <pattern>%shop@dir.su.edu.au
```

```
will match <pattern> in the lists of items sold by the
shop at the UCS.

"help" will produce this help.

e.g.     laserwriter%shop     will list all the products with
                  "laserwriter" in their name

--<Help Message edited>--
```

Now, finally, we can pose a query for powerbook accessories:

```
% finger powerbook%shop@dir.su.edu.au
[extra.ucc.su.oz.au]

--<Output edited>--
-----------------------------------------------------------
APPAY021 Mac PowerBook DUO Battery NiHy  $ 88.00    $ 104.00
```

CHAPTER 4

Navigating the Internet by Hand: Working with telnet

Her blue-tinted hair and grandmotherly demeanor belied Bernice's skill at looking things up. First hired to answer the phone, she now sat primly behind the computer terminal on her desk deftly fielding requests to find zip codes, names, addresses, longitude, latitude, congressional representatives, and library books.

- Hoping to discover the source of her information, curious co-workers asked her to find a book named **From Fish to Philosopher** in the library of a local medical school. Peering through her bifocals at the terminal, she typed `telnet nessie.cc.wwu.edu`. After some technical stuff appeared, she typed the word `LIBS` and the screen filled with a menu from which she selected "United States Library Catalogs." She passed through a menu of the fifty states to a menu of schools, where she found an entry for the local medical school. A short paragraph of instructions appeared, and after a brief dialog, she entered the title she was searching for. Almost instantly there was a description of the book, indicating that it was checked out.

- She smiled over her shoulder. "I'm afraid your book is checked out. Let's see if there's anything else of interest." She pressed two keys and the screen filled with a dozen entries. **From Fish to Philosopher** was midway down the screen. Books adjacent to it on the shelf were listed by author, title, and call number.

- Bernice was using `LIBS`, a standalone program developed by Mark Resmer at Sonoma State University in California. `LIBS` provides menu-guided access to virtually everything on Scott Yanoff's `Internet Services List`. (Yanoff's list and how to get it were discussed in Chapter 3.) `LIBS`, however, was not installed on her computer. She used the `telnet` program to reach a computer named nessie where `LIBS` was running.

A Delicate Balance: Resources and Applications

The Internet has an ecology unlike any other. There are thousands of information resources on the Internet. (Yanoff's list alone summarizes several hundred of them.) There are millions of people using the Internet to reach these resources, and there are only a dozen or so client/server application tools to make the connection between people and resources. This ratio of applications to resources makes good sense: if every information source on the Internet had its own network application, learning to use the network really would be a monstrous task.

Hundreds of Internet resources (bulletin boards, library card catalogs, and databases of every sort) are implemented as conventional, stand-alone programs running on individual computers that happen to be attached to the Internet. These resources do not have network accessibility built into them. The tool that puts a network-wide audience in touch with such stand-alone resources is telnet.

Telnet is a network application that you can use to log in to one computer on the Internet from another. With telnet you can navigate around the Internet manually. Unlike ftp (which makes a connection strictly for the purpose of transferring files), telnet connections are general-purpose. The use you can make of a telnet connection depends more on what the remote computer has to offer than on any of telnet's features. You can use telnet to reach stand-alone applications or even client/server applications that are installed on other computers. Applications that are accessible by telnet may use special login names (similar to the "anonymous" login name often used with ftp). Some telnet-accessible applications use no login name at. You can also use telnet from any computer on the network to connect to any other machine for which you have a login. We'll discuss these scenarios shortly, but first, let's take a look at what telnet does.

How telnet Works

The telnet command itself is almost trivial: you need only a host-name or an IP address to identify the computer to which you want to connect. Once the telnet connection is established, you should be prepared to enter a login name and password that are valid for the computer you've reached. Don't expect that your login name and password from your home computer will be valid elsewhere. A minimal telnet session is shown in Listing 4.1.

listing 4.1:
a sample telnet session

```
% telnet optimism.wsqpd.com
Trying 130.214.50.59 ...
Connected to optimism.
Escape character is '^]'.

SunOS UNIX (optimism)

login: bennett
Password:
Last login: Mon Jul 19 01:28:55 from xymd1b
SunOS Release 4.1.3 (GEN_CLIENT_413_SM64) #1: Thu Nov 5 15:41:03 PST 1992
TERM = (hds) vt100
optimism-% who
bennett  ttyp2   Jul 19 01:29 (optimism)
optimism-% logout
Connection closed by foreign host.
```

The computer from which you execute the telnet command (a client program) is the local computer. The computer to which a connection is made is the remote computer. In Listing 4.1, the remote computer is optimism.wsqpd.com and it has a login account named "bennett." The name of the local computer and your local user name don't play any role in making a telnet connection. Once you've connected to the remote computer, you can use it interactively. Here, we simply wanted to show the similarity between normal logins and logins through telnet; more often, as in this chapter's opening scenario, you'll use telnet for access to menu systems such as those provided by LIBS.

Telnet's Command Mode

Once you've made a connection via telnet (as discussed in the accompanying sidebar), you will be working with programs on the remote computer. Any commands you issue will be acted on by the

INPUT MODE: SEEING THROUGH TELNET - - - - - - - - - - -

For telnet to make a connection, the remote computer must be running a telnet server that listens for connection requests from telnet clients. (When telnet was developed, server programs running continuously in the background were referred to as daemons. The telnet server is usually named telnetd, a shortened form of *telnet daemon.*) On most Internet hosts, the telnet daemon is started automatically as part of the system's boot procedure.

Once a telnet client has connected to the server on a remote machine, they create a "virtual terminal" that enables you to work directly with programs running on the remote computer. Even though you can't see them, the telnet client and server are still there. They have become "transparent." Telnet creates the appearance that the terminal you're working on is connected directly to the remote computer.

The terminal connection may be simulated, but the interaction is certainly real. When you make a telnet connection to a UNIX computer, for example, your telnet session will show up among the currently logged-in users reported by the who command, as illustrated in Listing 4.1. (An ftp connection, for example, does not show up in the output of who.) However, telnet connections are not as direct as they appear. After making a remote application, not `telnet`. You can jolt `telnet` out of this "transparent" mode and into "command" mode by typing the `telnet` escape character. Control-] is the default, but (as you'll see in a moment) you can change this if need be. `Telnet` displays a reminder about the escape character at the start of each `telnet` session (see Listing 4.1 for an example). The signal that you're in command mode is the `telnet>` prompt. If you have an open connection to a remote computer, you can exit `telnet`'s command mode (and return to input mode) by just pressing the Enter or Return key in response to the `telnet>` prompt.

connection, the `telnet` client program passes anything you type across the network to the `telnet` server. The server on the remote computer starts a program (usually the same program used to prompt native users on the remote computer for login information). Any input the server receives from you via the `telnet` client is passed on to this program. Any output from the program is handed to the `telnet` server, which pushes it across the network to the `telnet` client, which finally passes the output through to you.

Your input and the program's output are passed back and forth by client and server until you log out of the remote computer. Logging out signals the `telnet` server that the session is over, and it closes the connection with the client. The client sees the closed connection, cleans up, and exits—returning you to the program (usually a shell or command interpreter) from which you called `telnet`.

Anything that can be done over a terminal connected directly to the remote computer can also be done through a `telnet` connection. From within a `telnet` session, you can even `telnet` from the remote computer to a third computer elsewhere on the network.

Telnet's command mode provides tools to manage the connection you have to the remote computer. If you intend to use "nested" telnet sessions, it is a good idea to assign a unique escape character to each of the sessions. The frequently-used telnet commands are summarized below, and an annotated telnet session illustrating the use of these commands appears in Listing 4.2. To see the on-line documentation available for telnet from a UNIX prompt, type man telnet.

? [*command*]	The ? command prints telnet's help messages. With no arguments, it prints a summary of all telnet commands. If you specify a command, telnet will display the help information for that command only.
open *hostname*	The open command attempts to make a connection to the named host. *Hostname* can be either a fully-qualified domain name or an IP address. Note that a telnet client can support only one open connection at a time.
close	The close command closes the current connection and returns to telnet's command mode.
quit	The quit command closes the current connection and exits telnet.
status	The status command displays the current status of telnet, including the name of the remote computer you're connected to. After a status command, you are returned to input mode if your telnet session has an open connection.

set escape	The set escape command can be used to
value	change the character that triggers
	command mode.

listing 4.2:
telnet Commands in Use

```
% telnet    Note no host name. Telnet will start in command mode.
telnet> status    From command mode, issue status command.
No connection.
Escape character is '^]'.
telnet> set escape ~    Change the escape character to '~'
escape character is '~'.
telnet> open optimism.wsqpd.com    Open a connection to opti-
mism.wsqpd.com
Trying...
Connected to optimism.wsqpd.com.
Escape character is '~'.

DYNIX(R) V3.1.0  (optimism)

login: bennett    Normal login sequence
Password:    Password not echoed

TERM = (vt100)
% who    "who" shows the telnet login
bennett  ttyp4  Jul 17 09:03
%    Escape character (~) is not echoed!
telnet> status
Connected to optimism.wsqpd.com.
Operating in character-at-a-time mode.
Escape character is '~'.    Telnet returns to input mode after status.
%    Press Return for prompt.
telnet> close    Escape to command mode and close the connection.
Connection closed.
telnet> status
No connection.
Escape character is 'é.
telnet> quit    Exit the telnet client.
```

Telnet and Other Applications (or When to Use telnet)

Telnet comes in handy in three circumstances:

- When you need access to a stand-alone application that is installed on another computer.

- When you want to use one of the Internet's client/server applications but don't have a client program installed on the machine on which you usually work.

- When you have a login on a remote computer and want to do some work on that host.

In any list of Internet services, you will find services and resources that are accessible via telnet. To use such a resource, you need only know the name (or IP address) of the computer on which it resides and a valid login name and password for that computer. Most services that rely on telnet access also provide a special login name that anyone can use to connect to the service. This is similar to the "anonymous" login with ftp, but each service available through telnet assigns login information independently.

In previous chapters we introduced archie (an application to locate files accessible via anonymous ftp). You can also use telnet to connect to the archie database. This is particularly useful if you have a number of archie queries. If the client program for archie is not installed on the Internet host you use, your only access to this service may be through telnet. The LIBS application, introduced at the beginning of this chapter, is a stand-alone tool that is accessible only through telnet. We'll discuss both of these in turn.

Using archie through telnet

The archie application, introduced in Chapter 3, is a tool for getting information about files that you can copy through anonymous ftp. The information about these ftp archives is stored in a database that can be queried through archie client programs or electronic mail. You can also query the archie database by using telnet to log in to any of the computers on which archie servers are running. (See Chapter 3 for a list of computers hosting archie servers.) Telnet connections to archie servers are helpful if several queries will be needed to produce the results you want. A telnet session for using archie is shown in Listing 4.3.

listing 4.3:
Using archie via a telnet Session

```
% telnet archie.unl.edu
Trying 129.93.1.14...
Connected to crcnis2.unl.edu.
Escape character is '^]'.

SunOS UNIX (crcnis2)

login: archie
Last login: Sat Jul 17 01:02:04 from pogo.den.mmc.com
SunOS Release 4.1.2 (CRCNIS2) #1: Wed Dec 16 12:10:12 EST 1992

    Welcome to the ARCHIE server at the University of Nebraska - Lincoln.

        Please report problems to archie-admin@unl.edu. We encourage peo-
ple to use client software to connect rather than actually logging in.
Client software is available on ftp.unl.edu in the /pub/archie/clients
directory.

    If you need further instructions, type help at the unl-archie>
prompt.

unl-archie> prog factbook
# matches / % database searched:     33 /-12%
```

```
Host bric-a-brac.apple.com    (130.43.2.3)
Last updated 01:47 26 May 1993

    Location: /alug
      DIRECTORY rwxr-xr-x        512  May 14  1992    factbook
<output truncated>
...
unl-archie> quit
Connection closed by foreign host.
```

The machines running archie servers are set up to respond to the host name archie. The archie hostname is an alias registered with the Internet Domain Name Service. (See the discussion of domain names in Chapter 2 for more information about assigning several names to the same computer.) For example, one of the sites running an archie server is the University of Nebraska at Lincoln (unl.edu). When you telnet to archie.unl.edu, as in Listing 4.3, telnet gives you the computer's unaliased name (in this case crcnis2). To make things simple, the archie servers also recognize the login name archie. To query the archie database, log in as archie (the archie account has no password).

When you log in to an archie server, you should see a message describing the service you're about to use. Read the opening message carefully. It will describe how to get help during the current session and how to report any problems you encounter. Archie's on-line help for telnet users is extensive.

The telnet version of archie uses the command prog to request a search. To search the archie database for filenames and directory names containing the keyword "factbook," for example, use the following command in response to the archie prompt:

```
unl-archie> prog factbook
```

Archie will respond to your queries with a progress report indicating the number of entries that satisfy your query and the percentage of the database searched so far.

Archie is a very heavily used Internet service, and telnet connections (unlike the connections of archie clients or the e-mail interface) are open-ended. They aren't closed until you deliberately close them. If, while connected via telnet to an archie server, you are interrupted and called away suddenly, leaving your telnet session in place would accidentally tie up resources that other people are eager to use. Consequently, the archie servers will accept only a limited number of telnet connections. Don't be surprised if you encounter an archie server that cannot accept a new connection, as in Listing 4.4.

listing 4.4:
Connecting to an Overloaded archie Server via telnet

```
% telnet archie.sura.net      archie.sura.net is a popular site.
Trying 128.167.254.195.
Connected to yog-sothoth.sura.net.
Escape character is '^]'.

SunOS UNIX (yog-sothoth.sura.net)

login: archie
Last login: Sat Jul 17 01:03:11 from sage.cc.purdue.e
SunOS Release 4.1.3 (NYARLATHOTEP) #3: Thu Apr 22 15:26:21 EDT 1993
Sorry, there are too many people already logged on.   This archie serv-
er is overloaded!
You can log in as qarchie which uses the prospero server to do
searches.
Telnet to archie.sura.net and log in as user qarchie.    There is an al-
ternative client.
The following is a list of other archie servers:
    archie.rutgers.edu         128.6.18.15     (Rutgers University)
    <listing truncated>
```

Using telnet to Reach Stand-alone Applications: LIBS

At the beginning of this chapter we described the use of LIBS, a telnet-accessible, stand-alone application that provides a convenient interface to many Internet resources. (LIBS is one of several such applications. Another similar service that is mentioned in Yanoff's Internet Services List resides on wugate.wustl.edu. To use that service, telnet to wugate.wustl.edu and log in as services.)

The resources for which LIBS provides an interface can all be accessed without going through the LIBS application. However, packaging access to so many Internet services in a single menu system is undeniably convenient, and you may find that using LIBS is easier than remembering the procedures for connecting to services that you don't use often. Access information for several LIBS sites appears in the Internet Services List. We'll use the LIBS application running on nessie at Western Washington University (nessie@cc.wwu.edu). Listing 4.5 shows how you use this information to reach LIBS via telnet.

listing 4.5:
Connecting to a Computer Running the LIBS Application

```
% telnet nessie.cc.wwu.edu    Telnet command with fully qualified domain name.
Trying...
Connected to nessie.cc.wwu.edu.
Escape character is '^]'.   Note escape character to toggle command mode.
VAX/VMS V5.4    @Nessie.cc.WWU.edu   Nessie is a VAX computer running VMS.
Username: LIBS  Enter the login name LIBS. Note that we aren't prompted for
a password.
Terminal Device_type set via /inquire to: VT100
   15-JUL-1993 21:19:58
--< Additional Credits truncated >--
                        Modified for WWU

          LIBS - Internet Access Software v2.0
      Mark Resmer, Sonoma State University, Dec 1992
                  WWU rev. 5/17/93

      On-line services available through the Internet:
      1 United States Library Catalogs
      2 Library Catalogs in other countries
      3 Campus-wide Information Systems
      4 Databases and Information Services
      5 Wide-area Information Services
```

```
6 Information for first time users
7 Special Internet Connection List

Press RETURN alone to exit now or
press Control-C Q <return> to exit at any time

Enter the number of your choice:
```

When you log in as LIBS, the LIBS program starts automatically. The top level LIBS menu has entries for several categories of Internet services. It also provides instructions for exiting from the program. When you exit from LIBS, you will be logged out of the remote computer (nessie in this example), your telnet session will end, and you will be returned to the shell prompt on the local computer.

Further into the Internet with LIBS

Once you have reached the LIBS application, you have the opportunity in a single telnet session to branch out easily and quickly from LIBS to other Internet resources. LIBS will handle the details of making connections for you, so you won't be forced to trust your memory or hunt around for a list of Internet services, and telnet will work discreetly in the background maintaining your connection to LIBS. Let's look at two examples of how LIBS executes commands for you within a telnet session.

A Simple Example: The Time Service

Once LIBS starts, you can browse through the various menus it displays without actually using any of the services it describes. Whenever you select a menu item that will connect to some resource outside of LIBS itself, LIBS displays a short description of the resource and hints for using it. Listing 4.6 shows how to move through the LIBS menus to use the National Bureau of Standards Time service.

(All this service does is accept incoming connections, display the current time as reported by the National Bureau of Standards reference clock in Colorado, and disconnect.) This dialog begins after we've selected item 4, Databases and Information Services, from the main LIBS menu shown in Listing 4.5.

listing 4.6:
Using the National Bureau of Standards Time Service via LIBS

```
Information services/databases in the following areas are accessible:
                1 Agriculture
                2 Arts/Humanities
                3 Business/Economics
                4 Education
                5 Entertainment/Games
                6 Scientific
                7 Weather/Time/Earthquakes
                8 Other Services
                Press RETURN alone to see previous menu
                Press Control-C Q <return> to exit at any time
                Enter the number of your choice: 7

The following information is available:
                1 Auroral Activity
                2 Earthquake Information Service
                3 National Bureau of Standards Time Service
                4 Tropical Storm Information
                5 Weather Information (University of Michigan)
                Press RETURN alone to see previous menu
                Press Control-C Q <return> to exit at any time
                Enter the number of your choice: 3

National Bureau of Standards Time Service
This service will give you the current time as read from the National
Bureau of Standards reference clock in Colorado Springs.
Do you want to connect now? (Y or N): y
Trying... Connected to INDIA.COLORADO.EDU, a SUN3 running SUNOS 4.0.
Sun Jul 18 16:54:24 1993
Connection closed by Foreign Host
Press <return> to continue:
```

Here's a summary of the steps:

1. From the LIBS top level menu, we chose the Databases/Information item.

2. The submenu for databases contains an item for weather, time, and earthquake information, and that menu contains an item for querying the National Bureau of Standards Time Service.

3. When this item is selected, LIBS explains briefly what kind of service is offered and asks for confirmation before connecting.

4. When you confirm that LIBS should connect to the time service, a telnet connection is opened between the machine LIBS is running on (nessie) and a machine named india at the University of Colorado.

5. The program that is run over that connection sends the current time and immediately closes the connection. This nested telnet session does its work and exits without disturbing the original connection to nessie.

Using LIBS as an Interface to telnet

Many of the services accessible through LIBS are interactive services (bulletin board systems, databases, etc.) in their own right, and you could connect to these directly with telnet without using LIBS. Using LIBS to connect to these interactive services has some distinct advantages: LIBS provides menus to guide you to the resources you're interested in, it keeps track of the information needed to make the telnet connection so you won't have to look up the FQDN for the service, and before LIBS runs telnet for you, it provides additional instructions for exiting from the service you've connecting to. When LIBS connects you with an interactive service via telnet, you'll work with that service as though you made the connection yourself.

Each interactive service behaves by its own rules. A good interactive service will provide—on-line—all the information you need to use the service. Many of the interactive services require users to register. When you connect to a library catalog or bulletin board service, you should be ready to provide some information about yourself. Registering protects the security of the service and enables the service providers to know their audience.

The U.S. Food and Drug Administration (FDA) maintains a bulletin board that is typical of interactive services on the Internet. You can reach it through either telnet or LIBS. The telnet command to reach the FDA Bulletin Board is this:

```
% telnet fdabbs.fda.gov
login: bbs
```

The FDA BBS can be reached from LIBS through the Database/Information submenu. Choose the Scientific menu item from the Information services menu. The menu of resources on scientific questions contains 18 entries. The FDA BBS is item 4. Listing 4.7 shows a session using this database.

listing 4.7:
Using the FDA bulletin board service via LIBS
─ ─ ─ ─ ─

```
Scientific Databases/Information Systems:
   1 American Mathematical Soc        2 Brookhaven National Lab
   3 Environmental Protection Agency  4 Food and Drug Agency
   5 GenBank                          6 Global Land Information System
   7 Lunar and Planetary Institute    8 MEDINFO
   9 NASA Extragalactic DB           10 NASA News Service
  11 NASA Spacelink                  12 National Nuclear Data Center
  13 National Space Data Center      14 NSF Info
  15 Southwest Research Institute    16 Supernet International
```

```
 17 US Naval Observatory              18 World Ocean Circ
            Press RETURN alone to see previous menu
            Press Control-C Q <return> to exit at any time
            Enter the number of your choice: 4
```

Food and Drug Agency
This database covers areas including: News releases, Enforcement Re-
port, Drug and Device Product Approvals list, Centers for Devices and
Radiological Health Bulletins, Text from Drug Bulletin, Current Infor-
mation on AIDS, FDA Consumer magazine index and selected articles, FDA
Federal Register Summaries by Subject, Summaries of FDA information,
Index of News Releases and Answers, FDA Federal Register Summaries by
Publication Date, Text of Testimony at FDA Congressional Hearings,
Speeches Given by FDA Commissioner and Deputy, Veterinary Medicine
News, Upcoming FDA Meetings, and Import Alerts.

Note the following instructions carefully
Once you are connected:
login: bbs <return> (must be in lower case!)
The first time you log in, you will be taken through a registration sequence.

Press Control-C Q <return> to exit at any time

Do you want to connect now? (Y or N): **y**
Trying... Connected to FDABBS.FDA.GOV.
 UNIX System V R.3 (WINS) (FDABBS)
login: **bbs**
UNIX System V Release 3.2.3 AT&T 3B2
FDABBS
Copyright (c) 1984, 1986, 1987, 1988, 1989, 1990 AT&T
All Rights Reserved
Login last used: Sun Jul 18 18:40:19 1993
```
           @@@@@  @@@@@@    @
           @      @    @  @ @               THE FDA
           @@@@@  @      @ @@@@@   ELECTRONIC BULLETIN BOARD
           @      @@@@ @ @    @
```
    Welcome to FDA's electronic bulletin board, a service of the Food
and Drug Administration.
            UNAUTHORIZED USE IS PROHIBITED BY TITLE 18 OF U.S.C.
Please enter your name (first and last) ==> **bennett falk**
Hello BENNETT FALK
Is this your correct name ? (Y/N): **y**
Please enter your password ==>
Welcome Back! Your last login was: 06/20 22:48:23
FOR LIST OF AVAILABLE TOPICS TYPE TOPICS

```
OR ENTER THE TOPIC YOU DESIRE ==>topics
     TOPICS       DESCRIPTION
  *  NEWS         News releases
  *  ENFORCE      Enforcement Report
  *  APPROVALS    Drug and Device Product Approvals list
  *  CDRH         Center for Devices and Radiological Health
  *  BULLETIN     Text from Drug Bulletin
  *  AIDS         Current Information on AIDS
  *  CONSUMER     FDA Consumer magazine index and selected articles
  *  SUBJ-REG     FDA Federal Register Summaries by Subject
  *  ANSWERS      Summaries of FDA information
  *  INDEX        Index of News Releases and Answers
  *  DATE-REG     FDA Federal Register Summaries by Publication Date
  *  CONGRESS     Text of Testimony at FDA Congressional Hearings
  *  SPEECH       Speeches Given by FDA Commissioner and Deputy
  *  VETNEWS      Veterinary Medicine News
  *  MEETINGS     Upcoming FDA Meetings
  *  IMPORT       Import Alerts
  *  MANUAL       On-Line User's Manual
FOR LIST OF AVAILABLE TOPICS TYPE TOPICS
OR ENTER THE TOPIC YOU DESIRE ==>index
YOUR CURRENT TOPIC: FDA_INDEX
TYPE QUIT TO LOGOFF OR TYPE HELP FOR AVAILABLE BBS COMMANDS
PLEASE ENTER A BBS COMMAND ==> quit

Connection closed by Foreign Host
```

As with the Time service discussed above, LIBS uses telnet to connect to the FDA BBS. Just as if you were using telnet to access the FDA directly, when you use the indirect LIBS method, you will be presented with a login prompt from the computer that hosts the database. When you log in as bbs, the bulletin board software will start and you will be asked for your first and last names. If you're new to the system, you will be asked to register. After registering, you will be presented with a list of topics about which the system has information. Once you've selected a topic, you can list and read any documents associated with that topic.

Ecological Considerations

At the beginning of this chapter, `telnet` was introduced as a tool to give an Internet-wide audience access to stand-alone information resources. `Telnet` is a necessary part of anyone's Internet toolkit. It is relatively easy to use, and many Internet resources would not be accessible at all without it. As you can see from the example of LIBS, `telnet` can be made even more convenient when it is embedded within a menu-driven application. The application frees the user from having to remember machine names and login information for resources of interest.

But `telnet` also needs to be used with some care. In most cases, a connection established with `telnet` will remain open until it is closed by the user who initiated it. The accumulation of open but inactive connections can utimately put a resource out of reach for anyone trying to make a new connection. Special-purpose client/server applications (such as `archie`) tend to manage their connections more efficiently than `telnet` does, and these clients should be preferred over `telnet` as a vehicle for launching database queries.

 HUNTING THROUGH THE INTERNET

Question   At the beginning of Chapter 4, Bernice was asked to look up information about *From Fish to Philosopher*. This is a real book. Who wrote it? For extra credit, who directed the movie made from this book?

Answer   The author of <u>From Fish to Philosopher</u> is William Homer Smith. The film was directed by Norman Laden.

To find the author's name, you could use the same strategy that Bernice used:

1. `Telnet` to `nessie.cc.wwu.edu` and login as `libs`.
2. Select U.S. Libraries from the menu of topics.

3. Select a state from the menu of states.

4. Select a library from the menu of school libraries.

5. When connected to the library of choice, perform a title search for From Fish to Philosopher.

Procedures for searches by title will vary from library to library. You'll have to use the on-line help at the library you connect to for tips on how to search by title.

An alternate method (which will also score bonus points for finding the director of the film version) is to use `telnet` to connect to the Library of Congress database (Yanoff's list has a reference for this site).

```
--<Menus and query results edited for readability>--
% telnet locis.loc.gov
Trying...
Connected to locis.loc.gov.
Escape character is '^]'.
  L O C I S :  LIBRARY OF CONGRESS INFORMATION SYSTEM


        To make a choice: type a number, then press ENTER



    1   Library of Congress Catalog    4   Braille and Audio

    2   Federal Legislation            5   Organizations

    3   Copyright Information          6   Foreign Law



    *     *    *    *    *    *     *    *    *    *
    7   Searching Hours and Basics
    8   Documentation and Classes
    9   Library of Congress General Information
```

```
12    Comments and Logoff


        Choice:  1      Select item 1 for card catalog searches.
CHOICE   LIBRARY OF CONGRESS CATALOG FILE

   1       BOOKS: English language books 1968-,  LOCI

   2       BOOKS earlier than the dates above.   PREM

   3       Combination of files 1 and 2 above    (LOCI and PREM).

   4       SERIALS cataloged at LC .             LOCS

   5       MAPS and other cartographic items     LOCM

   6       SUBJECT TERMS and cross references     LCXR

   12      Return to LOCIS MENU screen.


        Choice:  3   We're unsure of the publication date, so select
item 3 to search for entries before and after 1968.


MONDAY, 08/09/93  10:58 A.M.
***You are now signed on to LOCI and PREM.
   READY FOR NEW COMMAND:
READY LOCIS:
find from fish to philosopher    query for the title.
PAGE from fish to philosopher
NUMBER OF HITS=2       FIND  MUMS      SEQUENTIAL RECORDS          1
TO 2


1  From fish to philosopher.
      Smith, Homer William, 1895-1962.
         From fish to philosopher.    1953
            LC CALL NUMBER: QH369.S58
53-7332
```

```
2  Fish to philosopher motion picture / Merck Sharp & Dohme Interna-
tional ;
    produced by Norman Laden & Associates ; producer, director, and
screenwriter, Norman Laden.
        Fish to philosopher...   1982   A/V
            NOT IN LC COLLECTION
82-700391

READY LOCIS: quit
```

CHAPTER

The Electronic
Post Office

A sea of cubicles stretched across the carpeted floor of a high-ceilinged warehouse now converted to office space. At one of the cubes a woman plopped down in a chair under a potted palm and logged in to the workstation on her desk.

- "Coming back from vacation is always the worst," she sighed to no one in particular.

- A janitor cleaning a cube across the aisle stopped to listen.

- "It's mathematics, really," she went on. "This cube is next to, what, eight other cubes? In a day you might work with all of the people in those cubes and maybe a dozen others face to face. On the phone, even with voice mail, you talk to maybe twenty other people. That's forty people a day. I mean, what kind of business can you do contacting only forty people a day?"

- "I, uh, couldn't rightly say," he ventured. Peering at the screen, she called up an electronic mail program.

- "But here," she patted the side of the monitor, "Here you get 80 to 100 messages a day, 140 if you're really busy, and you know you're doing something." Her mailbox reported 1486 messages, a two-week backlog. Her right hand began to make jittery movements with the mouse.

- "Hey," he stepped forward "Is this, like, one of those Cyberspace gigs?"

- Startled, she swiveled the chair, and stared at him over the tops of imaginary glasses. "Yeah, but in Cyberspace, there are no e-mail backlogs."

E-Mail: the Message and the Medium

Electronic mail (or e-mail) is the ability to send and receive messages via computer. It has become a staple of modern business life and may soon find its place in the home. E-mail is not unique to the Internet. If your computer is on a LAN at work, you probably have some way to exchange e-mail messages with co-workers whether your local network is on the Internet or not. Many sites that have no outside network connection send and receive electronic mail by calling other computers at regularly scheduled times over ordinary phone lines.

An Overview of E-Mail

Electronic mail is not like the other client/server tools we've examined. In fact, e-mail works more like the regular postal service. When you send e-mail, a file containing your message is forwarded from one computer to another until the destination is reached. By contrast, client/server applications like ftp and telnet create an "end-to-end" connection (similar to the kind of connection you have in a telephone conversation) between you and an Internet resource. As powerful as these applications are, however, they have a difficult time establishing end-to-end connections between networks using different protocols.

Because it is a store-and-forward service, e-mail is an extraordinarily versatile tool. With e-mail you can:

- communicate with other Internet users.

- use Internet applications that have a mail interface.

- communicate with users on networks that are connected to the Internet but which use protocols other than IP.

114

- use some Internet services without actually having an account on the Internet itself.

We'll discuss how to do these things with e-mail, but first let's look at what paths there are for getting e-mail access.

Access To E-Mail

If you work on a multiuser computer (for example, UNIX systems or VAX/VMS computers), or if your computer is connected to a local network, e-mail of some kind should be available to you. Even if your computer does not have an e-mail feed from another computer or network, you can get e-mail access by subscription. To use a subscription service, you will need a computer (or a terminal of some kind), a modem, and a telephone line on which you can call the subscription service. In general, subscription services don't provide home delivery of your e-mail; you will have to log in to the service's computer to send and read mail.

Several kinds of subscription service offer e-mail access. Certainly e-mail is one of the services that is bundled with the login accounts available from commercial Internet access providers. Most of the "online" services (America Online, CompuServe, Genie, The WELL), whether they're connected to Internet or not, provide e-mail along with bulletin board and conferencing facilities. And of course, telecommunications companies like MCI and Sprint offer e-mail–only subscriptions. If you know how to use e-mail wisely, however, you can use many of the Internet's other services from an e-mail–only subscription service.

The number of people with whom you can exchange messages depends entirely on how well connected your computer (or your subscription service) is. Whether your Internet access is direct or indirect, you can choose your e-mail correspondents from among the millions of people worldwide who also have Internet access.

The Mechanics of E-Mail

You use e-mail by running a *mailer* program on your local computer. This program sends the messages you compose and stores any mail you receive. Whatever type of computer you use to send and receive mail, you may have a choice of mailer programs. On UNIX systems, e-mail is a heavily used application, and the mailers available for UNIX tend to be rich in features. For details about any particular mailer, there is no substitute for reading the documentation. Mailers differ dramatically in user interface and in strategies for storing received messages, but the basic sending and receiving capabilities should be common in all of them.

Creating new messages is a three-step process. You compose the message, address it, and finally send it on its way. In practice, most mailers ask you to provide an address before you've written the message. Addressing e-mail is a matter of identifying the person (or group of people) to whom you're sending mail. Names alone should be adequate to send mail to people who use the same local network that you use. Some systems, such as CompuServe, use numbers rather than names to identify users, but the principle is the same.

If you're sending mail to people outside your local network, the address should include the name of the computer on which the addressee receives mail. The addressing conventions for mail between Internet users are relatively simple. To address mail to another Internet user, you need only provide a user name and a fully qualified domain name in this format:

```
username@name.domain.qualified.fully
```

What you say in your messages and how you compose them are almost entirely up to you. Most mailers provide very limited built-in text editing capabilities for composing messages. Many mailers provide a way for you to use a separate text editor to compose messages. If your message is more than a few lines long, you'll want to take advantage of this feature. You may also want to compose your message in an editor ahead of time and save it in a file that the mailer will import to form the body of your mail message. (The ability to import files is a feature that may vary quite a bit from one mailer to another.)

Unless your mailer explicitly supports sending and receiving binary files, you should avoid sending files that are not text (or ASCII) files. There are two reasons for this. Text files can be read by virtually any mailer. If you send a binary file of some kind, the addressee will need the appropriate software to read your message. In addition, because mail is a store-and-forward service, you can't predict what programs will handle your message along the way. If you send binary formatted mail, intermediate programs may not be able to transmit your messages accurately.

When you tell the mailer that the message is ready to be sent, it will compare the address with addresses it knows. If the mail is going to a local user, your message will be routed to that user's *mailbox*, a file that holds messages arriving for a particular user. If your mail must be handed off to another computer or network, the mailer will check the computer portion of the address, make some decisions about routing your message to its destination, and send the message on its way. When your message arrives at its destination, a mail server at the destination computer will put it in the appropriate mailbox, where it will stay until the recipient logs in and issues a command to read mail.

Sending Mail, A Sample Session

The standard mailer on UNIX systems is named `mail`, and a sample dialog for sending mail is shown in Listing 5.1.

listing 5.1:
sending mail from one Internet user to another

```
% mail rosebody@well.com
Subject: what's in a name?
Hi,
I'm curious. what is the significance of your login name?
thanks,
Bennett
.
Cc: bennett@wsqpd.com
%
```

In this example, mail is being sent to a user named rosebody at a computer named well.com (the Whole Earth 'Lectronic Link, known colloquially as the WELL). The address rosebody@well.com is all that is needed to send mail from anywhere on the Internet to the user rosebody at the WELL.

The UNIX `mail` command first prompts for a subject. In this example, the subject is "What's in a name?" If you don't want to enter a subject, just press Return, and you can begin entering the text of your mail message. Note that there is no prompt for this; you simply begin typing. There are practically no editing capabilities built in to the UNIX mailer. You can use the erase character (usually either Backspace or Delete) to back up a character at a time within a line, but that's about it. It's a good idea to use relatively short lines in mail messages. Don't expect the mailer to wrap lines for you. At any point if you want to stop editing the message and throw the text away, just type Ctrl-C. The mailer will ask you to confirm that you want to quit by typing Ctrl-C a second time.

When your message is complete, enter Ctrl-D or a period (.) on a line by itself to send the message. In Listing 5.1, the mailer has been configured to prompt for any users who should receive a carbon copy of the message. In this case, we've requested that a carbon copy be sent to the sender, bennett@wsqpd.com.

Reading Rosebody's Mail

A few seconds after this mail is sent, it will arrive in rosebody's mailbox at well.com. When rosebody logs in next (whether in a few minutes or a few days), there will be a message that new mail has arrived. Listing 5.2 illustrates the process of reading mail.

listing 5.2:
reading and replying to mail on the Internet
_ _ _ _ _

```
well 1: mail
Mail version 5.2d (word-wrap) 9/22/91. Type ? for help.
"/usr/spool/mail/rosebody": 1 messages 1 new
> N 1 bennett@wsqpd.com Sun Aug 1 14:51 17/540 "what's in a name?"
& 1
Message 1:
From wsqpd.com!bennett Sun Aug 1 14:51:29 1993
Date:      Sun, 1 Aug 1993 14:52:12 -0700
From:      bennett@wsqpd.com (Bennett Falk)
To:     rosebody@well.com
Subject: what's in a name?
Cc:      bennett@wsqpd.com

Hi,
I'm curious. what is the significance of your login name?

Thanks,
Bennett

& r
To: rosebody@well.com bennett@wsqpd.com
Subject: Re: what's in a name?
Cc: bennett@wsqpd.com
```

```
Actually, it's a name I made up for a fictional
character a long time ago. The name was just on
my mind when I registered with the well. It never
occurred to me that anyone would read any significance
into it.

Thanks,
-rosebody
.
Cc: bennett@wsqpd.com
& d
& q
well 2:
```

To read mail using the UNIX mailer, you simply type mail and press Return. You'll see information about your version of mail, and about the messages in your system mailbox. The > symbol indicates the current message, and the letter N shows that this message is New. The number following that is the sequence of the message in the mailbox. These items are followed by the sender's name, the time the message was sent, the size of the message and the subject. The ampersand (&) is the mail command prompt; the program is now ready for your input. To read the current message, simply press Return. You can read any message by typing its sequence number.

Notice that the message now includes a header explaining who the message is from. You can respond to the current message by typing r at the mailer prompt. The mailer will compose an address and subject line for the response and begin accepting the text of your response. Editing the response is just like editing a new message. When you've completed the message, type Ctrl-D or a period on a line by itself. In Listing 5.2, the mailer rosebody is using automatically picked up the carbon copy list from the original message.

✖ TIP

Know your correspondents! Always check the "To:" and "Cc:" lists when replying to electronic mail to be certain your response is going to the audience you intend.

Rosebody, having responded to this message, issued a d command to delete it and then quit the mailer.

THOSE AWFUL MAIL HEADERS

New users of UNIX systems often have difficulty finding the text of mail they receive because it is buried under a wealth of header information in which they have no interest. This, for example, is the header that accompanied rosebody's reply:

```
From rosebody@well.sf.ca.us Sun Aug 1 14:54:31 1993
Return-Path: <rosebody@well.sf.ca.us>
Received: from nkosi.well.sf.ca.us by mail.wsqpd.com (5.65/SMI-
4.1/Netcom)
          id AA04961; Sun, 1 Aug 93 14:54:30 -0700
Received: from well.sf.ca.us (well.sf.ca.us [192.132.30.2]) by
nkosi.well.sf.ca.us (8.5/8.5) with SMTP id OAA21258; Sun, 1 Aug
1993 14:57:20 -0700
Received: by well.sf.ca.us id <14097-2>; Sun, 1 Aug 1993 14:56:48 -
0700
From: Bennett Falk <rosebody@well.sf.ca.us>
To: bennett@wsqpd.com, rosebody@well.sf.ca.us
Subject: Re: what's in a name?
Message-Id: <93Aug1.145648pdt.14097-2@well.sf.ca.us>
Date:      Sun, 1 Aug 1993 14:56:38 -0700
Status: R

Actually, it's a name I made up for a fictional...
```

Not only does the header make the message more difficult to read, it also increases the space the message takes up in your mailbox. Fortunately, you can control the size of the header by telling the mailer to ignore fields in which you aren't interested. On UNIX systems, the best way to do this is to create a `.mailrc` file that will enforce any local configuration changes you want to make in the mailer's behavior. This file is a simple text file that should be kept in your home directory. To cut the header information down to something manageable, put the following lines in `.mailrc`:

```
ignore Received Message-Id Resent-Message-Id Status
ignore Mail-From Return-Path Via
ignore X-Mailer In-reply-to
```

Mail that arrives at your system mailbox will include the full header, but the fields you suppress with the "ignore" command will not be displayed when you read new messages and will not be saved with the message if you move it to a local mailbox.

Mailbox Management

Managing your mailbox is one of those important things no one tells you about until it's too late. When you receive new mail, it will be stored in your system mailbox. This file should be kept relatively small. Mail messages take up disk space. If everyone lets them accumulate in system mailboxes, there is some risk of running out of space for new messages. In addition, the more messages your mailbox contains, the harder your mailer must work when you read mail. When software works hard, it usually also works more slowly.

Many systems automatically move mail messages from the system mailbox to a local mailbox after the message has been read. This protects the system mailboxes from running out of space, but at the cost of creating a local file that must also be managed.

The UNIX `mail` program, for example, by default puts messages that have been read but not otherwise disposed of in a file named `mbox` in your home directory. If you don't get into the habit of deleting messages (or saving them elsewhere), your `mbox` file will happily keep growing. If you're sure there's nothing you want to preserve in this file, it can be deleted. You may, however, want to delete messages from it selectively. The `mail` program can be used to browse through the `mbox` file with the following command:

```
% mail -f mbox
```

The mailer will provide a summary display of the messages in `mbox`, and you can read, reply to, delete or save messages just as you do when working with your system mailbox.

Finding Correspondents

At first glance, you might think that the usefulness of e-mail depends mainly on who, among Internet users, you know well enough to send messages to. In fact, there is a lot more to e-mail than sending mail to people you already know. For example, look at this piece of mail:

```
% mail sales
Subject: Competitive info needed!!!

Friends,
I'm putting together a proposal to install 5000
of our deluxe "Papa 'Presso" coffee machines
in a nationwide chain of convenience stores.
We're bidding against the new "'Spress Express" microprocessor-
controlled units from Coffee Cosmos.
I need a benchmark to show that we can make a Caffe
Latte faster than they can.
```

```
~B1
Thanks in advance,
T. Backmatter
Cc: marketing
```

Notice that the two names of recipients ("sales" and "marketing") don't have the *username@domainname* format. These names are *aliases*, a shorthand way of addressing mail to a group of people. T. Backmatter's request will be distributed to all the members of the sales and marketing aliases without each individual recipient being named in the message. In general, your mailer should enable you to define your own aliases for groups of people you send mail to frequently. (Check the documentation for your mailer to see how this is done.) When you create an alias for your own convenience, you alone have access to it. If you are part of a LAN at work, you may have access to company-wide aliases ("sales" and "marketing," for example) that are maintained by your system administrator and are available for anyone in your company to use.

There are also aliases that anyone on the Internet can use; these are known as *mailing lists*. Internet mailing lists represent interest groups or topics of discussion; and there are mailing lists devoted to such diverse topics as aeronautics, bread, the latest operating system from Sun Microsystems, theology, and vampires. Some mailing lists are discussion groups (moderated and unmoderated), and some are simply distribution lists for announcements from some source (for example, the U.S. Food and Drug Administration or the White House).

You can retrieve a catalog of more than 1200 mailing lists (the "list of lists") by anonymous ftp: the file is /netinfo/interest-groups at ftp.nisc.sri.com. This list identifies each mailing list by name and includes a short description of the list and its subscription procedure. The file is updated quarterly.

✗ TIP

If you find a list you're interested in and want to subscribe, don't send your request directly to the mailing address for the list. This will distribute your inquiry to **everyone** on the mailing list, when you need to reach only the person who maintains the list. Many lists have a separate address for administrative issues. Check the "list of lists" for subscription information. By convention, many administrative mailboxes use the suffix `-request` appended to the mailing list address. For example, if you're interested in a mailing list named `salamanders@wsqpd.com` your subscription request should be sent to `salamanders-request@wsqpd.com`.

Using Services through E-Mail

On the Internet, electronic mail is more than a medium for communicating with other people. It is also a general-purpose tool for querying databases and transferring files. We hinted at these more adventurous applications of mail by introducing mail-based name resolution services in Chapter 2 and the e-mail interface to `archie` in Chapter 3. Now we need to consider in more detail what happens when you use e-mail to interact not with other users, but with programs.

We'll look at three representative services:

- `Almanac` is an e-mail-based bulletin-board system for general information, agricultural issues, and market news. `Almanac` mail servers can be reached at a number of Internet sites. The example below will use the `almanac` mail server at `esusda.gov`.

- The `archie e-mail interface` enables mail-based querying of the database of `ftp` archives at any `archie` server.

- The `ftpmail` service (at `decwrl.dec.com`) provides an e-mail interface for file transfers via `ftp`.

For each of these services, we'll discuss how to contact it via e-mail, how to request its documentation, what its commands are, and what sort of e-mail you should expect in response. These and other e-mail services can be found in Scott Yanoff's Internet Services List. (Detailed instructions for retrieving this list via `ftp` are in Chapter 3.)

Mail-Based Bulletin Boards: The Almanac Service

The `almanac` service is an electronic bulletin board that users access via e-mail. It was developed at Oregon State University under a grant from the Kellogg Foundation, and there are at least six `almanac` installations around the continental U.S. To get started with `almanac`, send mail to the user `almanac` at one of the server sites. The body of the mail message should contain the command `send guide` to retrieve documentation for `almanac`. The message to reach `almanac` at the U.S. Department of Agriculture would look like this:

```
% mail almanac@esusda.gov
Subject: Almanac query...
send guide
send catalog
.
Cc:
%
```

Don't overlook the period on a line by itself at the end of your message. This is the signal to the mailer that your text is ready to send. In response to the `send guide` command, `almanac` will send you a message containing the manual (about 10 pages when printed). The manual describes `almanac` commands and how to use them, but it doesn't tell you what topics are available for discussion on this almanac server. The command `send catalog` returns a list of topics being discussed on this server. When you send both commands together, their combined output comes back in a single return message from the `almanac` server.

`Almanac` servers offer a diverse range of services. The USDA almanac server includes topics about the U.S. budget, national policy, and White House summaries. The catalog of primary topics also contains instructions for getting more detailed information about individual topics. For example, to get more detail on Economic Research Service Reports, mail `almanac` the command

`send ers-reports index`

`Almanac` will respond with a list of the reports it has on file and instructions for requesting e-mail copies of individual reports.

Each `almanac` server also contains a `mail-catalog` in which you'll find topic-oriented mail groups. (See Listing 5.3 for a sample listing of `almanac` mail groups.) Like other Internet mailing lists, the mail groups distribute messages about some topic to subscribers. Some `almanac` mail groups are forums inviting subscribers to participate in a discussion of some issue. Others are used to broadcast newsletters and reports to interested parties.

Listinɡ 5.3:
mail ɡroup listinɡ from an almanac server.

```
From almanac@oes.orst.edu Tue Aug 3 01:49:04 1993
Date: Tue, 3 Aug 93 01:51:53 -0700
To: bennett@wsqpd.com (Bennett Falk)
From: almanac@oes.orst.edu (Almanac Information Server)
Subject: RE: request
Reply-To: owner-almanac@oes.orst.edu
Status: R
```

```
--------
## Regarding your request:
 send mg catalog

              Almanac
          OES Mailing Groups Topic Catalog

      Oregon State University, Extension Service

Mailing-group archive available on OES.ORST.EDU.

To retrieve these documents, send the following request to
almanac@OES.ORST.EDU:

 > send mg <topic> <file>

<---informational messages deleted--->


              ---o---


Topic:     excuisine-mg
Title:     Extension Cuisine Mailing Group
Abstract:  This is the archive of mail sent to the excuisine-
           mg mailing-group at OES.ORST.EDU.

Topic:     extoxnet-mg
Title:     Extension Toxicology Mailing Group
Abstract:  Discussions relating to Extension toxicology.

Topic:     fdmktnews-mg
Title:     Food Market News
Abstract:  Newsletter on the trends and prices of food com-
           modities. Written by Mary Mennes of the University
           of Wisconsin and distributed nationally through
           Oregon State University Extension.

Topic:     forage-mg
Title:     Extension Forages Mailing Group
Abstract:  Discussion forum about forages.

Topic:     pie-mg
Title:     Public Issues in Education Mailing Group
Abstract:  Discussion forum for public issues in education.

Topic:     forage-mg
```

```
Title:      Mailing Group
Abstract:   Discussion forum.

Topic:      sod-mg
Title:      Mailing Group
Abstract:   Discussion forum.

<----Listing Truncated--->
```

The archie E-Mail Interface

Archie is one of the most versatile applications on the Internet, offering access via archie clients, telnet, and electronic mail. The basic service that archie provides is a database of anonymous ftp archives throughout the Internet. Anonymous ftp archives are files available for anyone to copy via an ftp client. (There is a detailed explanation of anonymous ftp in Chapter 3.) The archie database accepts queries containing keywords, and it returns the locations and names of files whose titles contain the specified keyword. The archie database is published to at least 10 sites, any of which can support queries via e-mail. (See Chapter 3 for a list of archie server sites.)

E-mail queries of the archie database should be addressed to the user archie at the computer named archie at one of the archie sites. For example, the e-mail address for the archie server at the University of Nebraska at Lincoln is archie@archie.unl.edu. A message to get usage information for the archie e-mail interface would look like this:

```
% mail archie@archie.unl.edu
Subject:
help
.
Cc:
```

There are a couple of nuances to the formatting of this message that you should be aware of. First, although the Subject line has been left blank, the `help` command could have gone there instead of in the body of the mail message. That's because when an `archie` server reads electronic submissions, it merges the subject line with the body of the message. Notice also that `help` is the only command in the message. `Archie` treats help commands as exclusive: once a help command is received in a message, the help message is sent, and all other commands in that message are ignored. Finally, notice that the `help` command begins at the left margin. Commands to `archie` servers must start in the first column of a line. If you indent the `archie` commands in your message, the server won't recognize them. `Archie` will respond with the help message to any incoming mail that contains no legal `archie` commands. The commonly used commands for archie's e-mail interface are listed below:

`help`

Returns usage information about archie's e-mail interface.

`prog` *pattern1* [*pattern2*, ...]

`Prog` is the basic search command used by `archie`. The arguments to the `prog` command are words or portions of words you expect to find in filenames at some `ftp` site. Archie will search for each pattern independently. If you use multiple patterns in a single `prog` command, all the results will be returned in a single mail message. If you use multiple `prog` commands, you will receive a separate message for each command. `Archie` uses the UNIX notion of "regular expressions" for its patterns. For more information about regular expressions, see the UNIX manual's discussion of the `ed` editor.

`site` *fqdn* or *IP address*

The `site` command requests a listing of the `ftp` archives at the specified site. You should use either a fully qualified domain name or an IP address for the site.

```
quit
```

The `quit` command tells the archie server to stop interpreting the input message.

Submitting An Archie Query By E-Mail

Let's test the e-mail interface to `archie`. Someone named John Chew is rumored to have created an e-mail address guide that summarizes how to address mail messages going from one network to another. This mail guide is supposed to be available through anonymous `ftp`, and if we can find it and download a copy of it, we can find out some things about networks attached to the Internet and how to exchange mail with them.

The first problem is to pick a keyword or pattern to submit in an `archie` command. "Internetwork," "mail," and "guide" are all promising candidates, but any of them alone will probably match many filenames in the `ftp` archives that we have no interest in; so we need to be more specific. The pattern we specify has to fit in one file name. On UNIX systems, file names frequently consist of two or more words, separated with dots (.), dashes (–), or underscores (_). Let's submit a mail query to `archie` using the pattern "mail-guide":

```
% mail archie@archie.unl.edu
Subject:
prog mail-guide
quit
.
%
```

An edited version of the response to this query is shown in Listing 5.4.

listing 5.4:
E-Mail Response to an archie query

```
From archuser@crcnis2.unl.edu Mon Aug 2 16:06:58 1993
Return-Path: <archuser@crcnis2.unl.edu>
Received: from crcnis2.unl.edu by mail.netcom.com (5.65/SMI-4.1/Netcom)
     id AA06318; Mon, 2 Aug 93 16:06:42 -0700
Received: by crcnis2.unl.edu (4.1/SMI-4.1)
     id AA08841; Mon, 2 Aug 93 18:57:35 EDT
Date: Mon, 2 Aug 93 18:57:35 EDT
Message-Id: <9308022257.AA08841@crcnis2.unl.edu>
From: archie@crcnis2.unl.edu
To: <bkf@netcom.com>
Subject: archie reply: prog mail-guide
Status: R

Sorting by hostname
Search request for 'mail-guide'

Host cs.columbia.edu (128.59.16.20)
Last updated 10:24 26 Jul 1993
 Location: /archives/mirror2/israel/network-info
     FILE     rw-rw-r--     8281 Oct 13 1992 inter-mail-guide.gz
...<Entries Deleted>...
Host ftp.nau.edu (134.114.64.70)
Last updated 00:50 6 Jul 1993
 Location: /internet
     FILE     rw-r--r--    24362 Apr 19 04:26 inter-net-mail-guide
```

The archie query returned a total of 25 references to sites having a file satisfying the "mail-guide" query. Most of the matches for this query were named either inter-net-mail-guide or inter-networking-mail-guide. Many of the sites reported were quite remote, and several had only compressed versions of the file. Still, there are several sites from which we can copy this file. One of the sites is ftp.nau.edu, and we'll work with that site in using ftpmail below.

Errors by E-Mail

Archie queries submitted by e-mail don't always go as planned. In a separate session, the query for files matching the "mail-guide" pattern was submitted via MCI-mail to the `archie` server at `rutgers.edu`. (We'll discuss the mechanics of sending mail between Internet and MCI-mail after we have retrieved a copy of the Internet Mail Guide.) This command ended with an `archie` server timeout error, and a notice of that error was sent back to the user who originated the query. The error notification is shown in Listing 5.5.

listing 5.5:
Error returned via E-Mail from an archie query

```
Command: read 1

Date:      Mon Aug 02, 1993 7:15 pm EST
From:      archie errors
           EMS: INTERNET / MCI ID: 376-5414
           MBX: archie-errors@dorm.rutgers.edu

TO:        * Bennett Falk / MCI ID: 601-9949
Subject: archie [prog mail-guide] part 1 of 1

>> path Bennett Falk <0006019949@mcimail.com>
>> prog mail-guide
# Error from Prospero server - Timed out (dirsend)
>> quit
```

The command prompt for the MCI-mail mailer program is `Command:`. In the MCI system the `read` command is used to display messages. Structurally, the message is very similar to UNIX e-mail. There is a short header with fields identifying the time the message was sent, the sender, the receiver, and the subject. The body of the message includes the text of the original query (the lines set off with >>), and the `archie` server error (the line set off with #). The message that reports the error gives us a chance to check the query that was submitted. In this case, there is nothing wrong with the query; something out of our control kept the server from responding in a timely way.

Ftp via E-Mail: Ftpmail

With archie's help, we've located a file that is of interest (/internet/inter-net-mail-guide at ftp.nau.edu). To retrieve a copy of that file, we'll use the ftpmail service, at decwrl.dec.com. Use this site for ftpmail if you're in North America. A separate site is available for European users. (Ftpmail was developed by Paul Vixie at the Digital Equipment Corporation's Western Research Laboratory.) As with many other things on the Internet, the first step in using ftpmail is to get ftpmail to tell us how to use it. We do this by simply sending a message containing the word "help" to ftpmail@decwrl.dec.com. Note that ftpmail will ignore the Subject line of your message.

```
% mail ftpmail@decwrl.dec.com
Subject:
help
quit
.
Cc:
%
```

The help message that is sent in response to this query includes a command summary, several usage notes about different features, and a number of examples. Frequently used ftpmail commands are summarized below:

reply *mailaddr*

Set return address to which files should be mailed.

connect *host*

Connect to the named host ("anonymous" is the default login name).

```
ascii
```

Files to be transferred are printable ascii.

```
binary
```

Files to be transferred are binary.

```
chdir directory
```

Change directory (only once per session).

```
compress
```

Compress binary files.

```
uuencode
```

Uuencode binary files before mailing.

```
chunksize size
```

Split files into size-byte sections for e-mail (default is 64000).

```
ls directory
```

Short listing of the named *directory*.

```
dir directory
```

Long listing of the named *directory*.

```
index pattern
```

Search for *pattern* in ftp server's index.

```
get file
```

Get the named *file* and have it mailed to you (max of 10 get commands per session).

```
quit
```

Terminate script, ignore rest of message.

Ftpmail uses chdir in place of ftp's cd command, and it has a number of commands that filter files (through compress, uuencode, and split) to make them suitable for e-mail. Apart from these differences, however, the commands for ftpmail are very similar to the standard ftp commands.

You can start an e-mail file transfer by sending ftpmail a message containing commands very much like those you would execute in an interactive ftp session. The following message instructs ftpmail to connect to ftp.nau.edu, move to the /internet directory, and retrieve the file named inter-net-mail-guide:

```
% mail ftpmail@decwrl.dec.com
Subject:
connect ftp.nau.edu
chdir internet
get inter-net-mail-guide
quit
.
Cc:
%
```

Shortly after this message is dispatched, ftpmail returns the first of several status reports. This report confirms that the request has been queued, repeats the commands contained in the request, and lets us know how many requests are ahead of us in the queue. It is not uncommon for the queue to contain several hundred jobs. Ftpmail's initial response to a request also contains some supplemental documentation explaining in detail what you can expect.

Ftpmail will make as many as five attempts to connect to the specified system. If it tries to connect and fails, you will receive a status message advising you of the failure and of the number of attempts still to be made.

When the transfer finally succeeds, you will receive the requested file as one or more mail messages (depending on the size of the file and the "chunksize" in effect for your transfer). You will also receive a status message describing the ftp session in which the file was transferred. Note that file transfers via ftpmail don't happen instantaneously. When John Chew's Internetworking Mail Guide was retrieved, roughly nine hours elapsed between request and completion.

Uuencode: Making Binary Files Mailable

Many of the files you'll find available through ftpmail are binary files. (The great divide between ASCII and binary files was introduced in Chapter 3.) "Binary" is an umbrella term for any file that contains data outside the ASCII character set, and it includes compiled programs, compressed files, and "archive" files produced with programs like PKZIP or the UNIX "tar" command. In their natural state, binary files don't mail well: mailers have a hard time transferring them intact. To remedy this problem there are two utilities (uuencode and uudecode) that are widely distributed on the Internet. These utilities were first developed in the UNIX environment, but there are now versions of them for other computers as well. Uudecode comes in particularly handy for PC users.

Uuencode produces an all-ASCII copy of a binary file. Uudecode translates files produced by uuencode back into their natural format. The command line for uuencode on a UNIX system looks like this:

```
% uuencode destname < filename > filename.uue
```

In this command, *filename* is the binary file you want to convert to ASCII. *Destname* is the name you want the file to have when it is eventually decoded at its destination. Ordinarily you'd use the file's original name for the destination name. The < *filename* part of the

command line tells uuencode to use *filename* for its input. The
`> filename.uue` on the command line tells uuencode to create a file
named *filename*.uue and put the ASCII version of *filename* there. After
you've done this, *filename*.uue is perfectly safe to mail.

When you receive a piece of mail that has been uuencoded (as you
might using `ftpmail`), you can use uudecode to convert the file back
to its binary format. When you receive a uuencoded file in e-mail, it
will look something like this:

```
% mail
Mail version 5.2d (word-wrap) 9/22/91. Type ? for help.
"/usr/spool/mail/rosebody": 1 message 1 new
>N 1 rosebody Thu Sep 9 08:14 109/6271 "UNIX Tuna"
& 1
Message 1:
From bennett@optimism.wsqpd.com Thu Sep 9 08:14:32 1993
To:     rosebody
Subject: UNIX Tuna
Date:      Thu, 9 Sep 1993 08:13:49 -0700

begin 644 unix_tuna.Z
M'YVO2-[<'>'D#'1#1#1#>'=>>>#--'----
M'YV02-[<'>'D#1T0=-'@#>-8'Y%='---
M#8@A@J=-@@#%-'PLd--'@P@j@@.&
M#3U@'>B@&@@@@@@@@@@@@@@@@@@@
MXQW1N#@@'&O&^^^@#@@@@@@@@@&
```

The line that reads `begin 644 unix_tuna.Z` is the start of the uuencoded message. When you decode this message, it will produce a file
named unix_tuna.Z. This is the destination name that was provided
to uuencode.

When you receive an encoded file in mail, save the message in a
file. When you quit the mailer, you can use uudecode on this file to
convert the message to binary. For example, if the message above was
saved in a file named tuna, the uudecode command would be uudecode
tuna. Here is the uudecode command sandwiched between two ls commands that show what files are present before and after uudecode.

```
% ls -l
-rw-r--r-- 1 rosebody well      6281 Sep 9 08:17 tuna
% uudecode tuna
% ls -l
total 12
-rw-r--r-- 1 rosebody well      6281 Sep 9 08:17 tuna
-rw-r--r-- 1 rosebody well      4336 Sep 9 08:18 unix_tuna.Z
```

Notice that uudecode doesn't remove "tuna." If uudecode succeeds, you can remove this file. One other point of interest is that tuna contains the message we received complete with all the header information that mail supplied. Uudecode ignored everything in the file up to the "begin" line. It is possible (but not very likely) that a mail header could interfere with uudecode. If that happens, the file you're decoding can be edited (in an ASCII editor, of course) to remove everything above the "begin" line. Be careful not to change or delete the begin line itself.

By the way, unix_tuna.Z is a compressed file. After decoding, it still needs to be decompressed to be usable. Decompressing looks like this:

```
% compress -d unix_tuna
% ls -l
total 15
-rw-r--r-- 1 rosebody well      6281 Sep 9 08:17 tuna
-rw-r--r-- 1 rosebody well      8165 Sep 9 08:18 unix_tuna
```

Notice that decompressing replaced unix_tuna.Z with unix_tuna.

Mail between Networks

Thus far, we've looked at e-mail primarily as an exchange of messages in which both sender and receiver are within the Internet. As large as it is, however, even the Internet has boundaries. Some of the Internet's points of contact with other networks can only be crossed by e-mail, and the familiar `user@host.domain` address format may not be adequate for mail delivery in a foreign network. John Chew's Inter-network Mail Guide discusses e-mail addressing for more than thirty different networks. Not all of these networks are of interest: some are private corporate networks, and some have no point of contact with the Internet. The accompanying sidebar summarizes e-mail address-ing conventions between the Internet and several of the networks with which Internet users commonly exchange mail.

 E-MAIL ADDRESSING BETWEEN NETWORKS - - - - - - - - - -

BITNET: To send mail from a BITNET site to an Internet user, use one of the following address forms:

user@host

or

gateway!domain!user

To send mail from an Internet site to a BITNET user, use the following address form:

`user%`*site*`.bitnet@`*gateway*

(Substitute for *gateway* the name of a host that serves both Internet and BITNET.)

CompuServe: To send mail from a CompuServe site to an Internet user, use the following address form:

`>Internet:`*user@host*

(Add the prefix `>Internet:` to the Internet address.)

To send mail from an Internet user to a CompuServe site, use the following address form:

```
71234.567@compuserve.com
```

(CompuServe user IDs are two numbers separated by a comma. Replace the comma with a period and add the domain name compuserve.com.) MCIMail: To send mail from an MCIMail site to an Internet user, use the following address form:

```
create <CR>
TO:  User Name
EMS: Internet
MBX: user@host.domain
```

To send mail from an Internet user to an MCIMail site, use one of the following address forms:

```
acctname@mci_mail.com
```

or

```
acct_id@mci_mail.com
```

(Account names may not be unique; MCI *acct ID* is a 7-digit number.)

SprintMail: To send mail from a SprintMail site to an Internet user, use the following address form:

```
    C:USA, A:telemail, P:internet, ID:user(a)host.domain
```

To send mail from an Internet user to a SprintMail site, use the following address form:

```
/PN=Bennett.Falk/O=co.wsqpd/ADMD=SprintMail/C=US@sprint.com
```

UUCP: To send mail from a UUCP site to an Internet user, use one of the following address forms:

user@host

or

gateway!domain!user

To send mail from an Internet user to a UUCP site, use the following address form:

user%host.UUCP@uunet.uu.net

What Are These Networks?

SprintMail and MCIMail are commercial e-mail services running on networks operated by Sprint and MCI, respectively. Sprint and MCI e-mail subscribers can send and receive mail with a local phone call anywhere in the United States. CompuServe is a commercial timesharing and conferencing system that also offers e-mail subscription.

BITNET is a world-wide network chiefly for educational and research institutions. It is home to discussion groups managed by the LISTSERV mailing-list manager.

The UUCP network is a loose association of computer sites that communicate via modems and phone lines using the UUCP (UNIX-to-UNIX Copy) protocol to transfer data. UUCP is essentially a store-and-forward network. It is also the home of the USENET News, which many people mistakenly believe to have originated on the Internet.

Interpreting Foreign Addresses on the Internet

Mail originating on the Internet tries to retain the `user@host.domain` format wherever possible. This is not always easy. There are intuitively satisfying Internet domain-style names (`compuserve.com`, `mci_mail.com`, `sprint.com`, etc.) for the commercial networks outside the Internet, but there is no single domain name for either BITNET or UUCP addresses. Addressing mail to one of these networks requires that you know an Internet host that serves as a gateway between the destination network and the Internet. (A gateway is a machine, connected to two different networks, that is capable of passing information back and forth between them.) For BITNET, `cunyvm.cuny.edu` is one such gateway. A UUCP network gateway is `uunet.uu.net`.

The addresses that route mail through a gateway have an unusual structure. Everything to the right of the @ is the gateway's Internet domain name. To the left of the @, a percent sign (%) is used to separate the user's name from the host name in the destination network. This *user%host* notation is interpreted when the message arrives at the gateway and is handed off to the destination network.

Each of the commercial services (CompuServe, MCIMail, and SprintMail) has a unique notation for identifying users. CompuServe uses two numbers separated by a comma. MCIMail uses both an account name and an account ID. Only the account ID is guaranteed to be unique. Finally, SprintMail identifies users with the notation proposed by the X.400 e-mail standard. This notation includes fields for personal name (PN), organization (O), and country (C). Once you know that SprintMail's user ID includes all these fields, it is a little easier to recognize that SprintMail addresses have a familiar structure:

```
a_very_long_user_name@sprint.com
```

Addressing Internet Users from Foreign Networks

Sending mail to the Internet from a foreign network is a little more straightforward, as you can see in the sidebar. Most foreign networks accept names in the user@host.domain format. UUCP and BITNET can deliver mail to Internet users with no further information. Users of the commercial networks should consult their documentation or on-line help to see how to indicate that Internet is the destination network. On CompuServe, you indicate that Internet is the destination network by adding the prefix >Internet: to the user@host name. SprintMail addresses include the destination network name in a field labeled P:. SprintMail also uses the format <user(a)host.domain>.

For MCIMail users, the destination network is specified in response to a prompt when creating mail. Listing 5.6 shows the procedure for MCIMail users to address mail to Internet users.

listing 5.6:
Addressing Mail to the Internet from MCIMail

```
Command: create

TO:     Thalamus Backmatter
        Thalamus Backmatter not found in the MCI Mail Subscriber Direc-
tory.
        You may enter an address for paper, telex, EMS or FAX delivery.

        0 - DELETE
        1 - Enter a PAPER address
        2 - Enter a TELEX address
        3 - Enter an EMS address
        4 - Enter a FAX address

Please enter the number: 3
Enter name of mail system.

EMS:    internet
  EMS 376-5414 INTERNET     MCI Mail     Downers Grove,
```

```
Enter recipient's mailbox information.

MBX:      backmatter@wsqpd.com

If additional mailbox lines are not needed press RETURN.

Subject: Hi, this is a test...

Text: (Enter text or transmit file. Type / on a line by itself to end.)

This was sent from mci-mail to the Internet.
Please reply when you get this.

thanks,
bennett
/
Handling:
Send? yes
One moment please; your message is being posted.

Your message was posted: Mon Aug 02, 1993 10:41 am EST.
There is a copy in your OUTBOX.

Command:
```

The Future of E-Mail

Mail is certainly here to stay. It is an extraordinarily useful tool for personal communication. It can be used as a networked application to bring resources within reach with relatively little overhead. It provides a medium for communications to be passed between networks.

However, the e-mail of the future will not be like the mail programs we use today. E-mail is now largely an ASCII medium, and messages with binary content must be massaged or filtered to be acceptable to mail. The e-mail of the future will have to deal transparently with binary messages. E-mail is still primarily a medium of the written word, yet it must ultimately be able to communicate with pictures and sound as well. E-mail is also relatively slow when compared with the performance modern client/server applications achieve. The e-mail of the future will have to deliver more data faster and in more pleasing ways.

With the addition of e-mail, your orientation to the Internet's basic tools is complete. For most of the Internet's history, users have gotten what they wanted from the Internet with these tools. It is unlikely that any of these tools will become obsolete, but the trend in Internet applications is to give these basic tools a more convenient interface. In Part III we'll look at some of these second-generation network applications.

🚗◀ HUNTING THROUGH THE INTERNET - - - - - - - - - - - -

Question I've heard about wireless cable TV, but this is a new field and I'm worried about doing business with people I don't know in a new industry. Where can I find out more?

Answer A first step is to see what is available through ftp:

```
% archie -s wireless
<--output truncated-->
Host plaza.aarnet.edu.au
     Location: /usenet/FAQs/rec.video.cable-tv
          FILE -r--r--r--      24768  Sep  3 06:59  Wireless_Ca-
ble_TV_FAQ
<--output truncated-->
```

This looks promising. It's a list of Frequently Asked Questions about Wireless Cable. Unfortunately, it's in Australia. We could get a copy from there, but we can probably find it closer to home. Now that we know what to look for, another archie search to look for "Wireless" (a case-sensitive search, this time) might help:

```
% archie -c Wireless

Host plaza.aarnet.edu.au
```

```
     Location: /usenet/FAQs/rec.video.cable-tv
          FILE -r--r--r--      24768  Sep  3 06:59  Wireless_Ca-
ble_TV_FAQ

<--Output Edited-->
Host athene.uni-paderborn.de

     Location: /doc/FAQ/rec.video.cable-tv
          FILE -rw-r--r--      10126  Sep  3 06:59  Wireless_Ca-
ble_TV_FAQ.gz

Host charon.mit.edu

     Location: /pub/usenet-by-group/rec.video.cable-tv
          FILE -rw-rw-r--      24768  Sep  3 06:59  Wireless_Ca-
ble_TV_FAQ
     Location: /pub/usenet-by-hierarchy/rec/video/cable-tv
          FILE -rw-rw-r--      24768  Sep  3 06:59  Wireless_Ca-
ble_TV_FAQ
<--Output Truncated-->
```

The entry from MIT looks promising. We can confirm that by downloading it via `ftp`:

```
% ftp charon.mit.edu
Connected to charon.mit.edu.
220 charon FTP server (Version 6.6 Wed Apr 14 21:00:27 EDT 1993)
ready.
Name (charon.mit.edu:bkf): anonymous
331 Guest login ok, send e-mail address as password.
Password:
230 Guest login ok, access restrictions apply.
ftp> verbose
Verbose mode off.
ftp> cd pub/usenet-by-group/rec.video.cable-tv
ftp> get Wireless_Cable_TV_FAQ
ftp> quit
```

This file is compiled by Brian Carlin, and contains the answers to the following questions:

We answered this question using only the tools we know about so far. In fact, this FAQ is part of a USENET newsgroup, and we could have gotten to this file in several different ways. Chapters 6, 7, and 8 will show you some alternate ways of retrieving this sort of information.

THE INTERNET COMMUNITY'S APPLICATIONS: GOPHER, WORLDWIDEWEB, AND NET NEWS

The growth of the Internet is changing the way people use it. The new generation of Internet applications (represented here by gopher and W^3) are designed to let you use resources without worrying about where they are on the network. These are applications that guide you to resources using menus or hypertext documents. In Chapter 6, you'll learn about gopher and the database that indexes gopher menu item titles. In Chapter 7, the WorldWide Web is introduced.

- Finally, in Chapter 8, you'll encounter the USENET News with more than 4000 discussion topics.

CHAPTER

6

Internet Access for the Armchair Explorer: gopher

"Chloe, are you playing with that Internet thing again? Do you have to spend so much time on that computer?" Chloe's mother Sarah stood in the doorway blocking the light from the hall. The 15-year-old spoke but did not look up. "It's not 'play', mom, I'm learning things. You should try this sometime, you'd like it."

- "I can't get interested in computers for their own sake, Chloe. If there were something of value, like a women's network or something, I might be interested." Sarah stepped into the room and sat on the bed. Chloe continued to look at the screen. "In a way, there is a women's network, you know," she said.

- "On the computer? I didn't know that," Sarah replied. "Where is it?" Chloe gave a command, and a menu appeared on the screen listing topics by and for women. She moved aside and offered her mother the chair. "There," she said, "This menu goes on for twelve screens, and all the items on it are women's items."

- Sarah scanned the menu. "Where did this come from?" she asked.

- "It's from all over the Internet. I just asked to see all the items that have 'women' in the title. They aren't all winners, and some are duplicates. But when you weed out the things you know you don't want to see, you can find the really interesting stuff a lot faster." But Sarah had already selected an item and was skimming through the text of a recent speech delivered by the First Lady.

What Gopher Is

If you are fascinated with the Internet's information resources but have a low tolerance for FQDNs, IP addresses, directory names, user names, passwords, and file types, the Internet gopher is the tool you've been waiting for. Technically, gopher is a "distributed document delivery system." Fortunately, it's much more appealing (and more fun to use) than that description makes it sound. In practice, gopher is something like an easy-to-use ftp without walls. That is, you can retrieve files via gopher without knowing which Internet host contains the file or what directory the file is stored in. The aim of the gopher application is to bring you information from all over the Internet as seamlessly as possible. Unlike any other application we've discussed so far, gopher doesn't require you to memorize a domain name or login information. You won't even have to remember which gopher server manages the information you want to retrieve. Gopher is so successful at hiding the boundaries between machines and servers that the term "Gopherspace" has been coined to refer to the complete pool of information resources managed by gopher servers throughout the Internet.

Because gopher is so easy to use, it has become an extremely popular vehicle for publishing information on the Internet. There are more than 750 gopher servers spread throughout the Internet. Many of these are devoted to specialized areas of interest. For example, there are at least five servers managing information on plant genome projects. Many businesses use gopher servers to reach the Internet audience. There is, for example, a gopher server for *The New Republic*. There are also gopher servers for nonprofit organizations and advocacy groups such as the Electronic Frontier Foundation (EFF). Apart from its advocacy work, the EFF gopher is host to a number of electronic periodicals that challenge the conventions of mainstream journalism. Gopher provides a congenial medium for these and many more activities.

Gopher was developed in 1991 at the University of Minnesota. The gopher development team there continues to work on enhancements and extensions of the system, and the UM gopher server remains the Mother Gopher. Unlike ftp, telnet, and mail, gopher is an application designed for the current state of the Internet. It assumes that there will be lots of users, that the users shouldn't be bothered by the details of managing client/server connections, that each connection from client to server should be as brief as possible, and that the physical network is fast enough to perform well even if the client program must open a connection for each query it sends to the server.

How gopher Works

When you run a gopher client program on an Internet host, it connects to a gopher server elsewhere on the Internet. By default, clients connect first to the Mother Gopher at the University of Minnesota, and from this connection you can maneuver from server to server throughout the Internet. If you know that the resources you're after are managed by a different gopher, you can bypass the Mother Gopher entirely and make your initial connection to the gopher that manages the data you're interested in. To do so, you need to supply the fully qualified domain name of the server's host and the port it monitors for connections. Port 70 is usually reserved for gopher servers. To start a gopher session with the server at the University of Nevada at Reno, use this command:

```
gopher gopher.unr.edu 70
```

(The UNR gopher has a particularly rich veronica database. You may want to refer back to this address during the discussion of veronica.)

After a connection is established, the client asks the server for a short listing of the resources it manages. The server's resources are organized hierarchically, usually in a tree-like directory structure. The first listing a server sends is the root level of this directory hierarchy. The client program formats the listing into a menu and displays it on your screen. When you select an item from this menu, the client relays your choice back to the server, and the server does whatever is appropriate for that kind of item. If the item you selected is a directory, the server sends back a listing of that directory's contents, and the client presents that to you as a menu. If your selection is a file, the server will send the client the contents of the file. When the client receives a file, it checks the file type and does whatever is sensible for a file of that type. If the file is text, the client displays it, and after you've looked at it, you'll have the option of printing, mailing, or saving the file locally. If the file is binary, the client will prompt you for a file name to use when saving the file locally.

Gopher Menus and the Objects Behind Them

At first glance, you might think that gopher is just a tool for browsing through files and directories. After all, it recognizes six different kinds of files. When file selections appear in a menu, gopher indicates what kind of file (ASCII, Binary, DOS Binary, etc.) or directory the item stands for. As you rummage through gopher menus, however, you'll find that many of the menu items point to resources outside the gopher server you've connected to. The files and directories that menu items point to may be on another Internet host elsewhere. In fact, a menu item on one gopher server may point to resources under another gopher's control. Some gopher servers contain no data at all, only links to other gopher servers. Your client program will deal equally well with both servers, and unless you ask for technical information about the menu item, you won't know which gopher server the resource is really located on.

Some gopher menu items are not files at all, but gateways to programs or to other application (that is, non-gopher) servers. Through a gateway menu item you could trigger a telnet session from your local computer to another machine across the Internet or request a keyword search on the contents of the current directory. A gopher menu item can represent any of a dozen different things, and most gopher menus include icons indicating what type of object each item represents. Internally, gopher uses single-character identifiers to name each object type. Most of the time the identifiers are safely out of view, but, as you'll see later, when you ask for information about an item, gopher displays the identifier without telling you what it stands for. The list of gopher objects, their identifiers, and icons appears in Table 6.1.

table 6.1: Gopher Objects, their Identifiers, and Icons

MENU ITEM TYPE	GOPHER IDENTIFIER	ICON
File	0	-none-
Directory	1	/
BinHexed Macintosh File	4	<HQX>
Uuencoded file	6	-none-
DOS Binary file	5	<PC Bin>
Binary file	9	<Bin>
Graphics File in GIF Format	g	<Picture>
Image File	i	<Picture>
Index Search	7	<?>
Telnet Session	8	<TEL>

table 6.1: Gopher Objects, their Identifiers, and Icons (continued)

MENU ITEM TYPE	GOPHER IDENTIFIER	ICON
Telnet 3270 Session	T	<3270>
CSO Phone-book Server	2	<CSO>
Error	3	-none-

A few of the objects Gopher recognizes may be new to you. Telnet 3270 is a special implementation of the telnet program to connect to IBM computers that use the 3270 "block mode" terminal. A CSO Phone-book Server is a tool for maintaining a campus-wide phone directory. Index Searches are used to retrieve files containing keywords that you specify. Gopher provides an interface to index searching tools of various kinds. One popular indexing and retrieval tool on the Internet is the Wide-Area Information Server (WAIS). WAIS itself isn't discussed in this book, but you don't need to know about WAIS in order to query WAIS indexes through gopher. Index searches are discussed in more detail later in this chapter. A sample menu showing menu items with icons appears in Listing 6.1.

listing 6.1:
A Sample gopher Menu Showing Different Item Types

```
              Internet Gopher Information Client 2.0


                        Sample   Menu

-->    1.   Plain File.
       2.   Listing of /tmp Directory  /
       3.   CSO phone-book server <CSO>
       4.   Macintosh BinHexed file <HQX>
       5.   DOS Binary File <PC Bin>
       6.   Index Search <?>
       7.   Telnet Session to optimism <TEL>
```

```
8.  Binary  File <Bin>
9.  Telnet to 3270-based host <3270>
10. Graphics file in GIF format <Picture>
11. Image file <Picture>
```

```
Press ? for Help, q to Quit, u to go up a menu
Page: 1/1
```

Getting Prepared to Use gopher: What You'll Need

To use gopher, all you need is Internet access and a gopher client program to run on the computer that provides your Internet connection.
If you're working on a UNIX system and using the terminal-based
version of the gopher client (as opposed to the version for a graphical
user interface like Xwindows), you'll need to know what kind of terminal you're using. Gopher is a "full-screen" application, and it needs
to know some features of the terminal you're working on. On many
Internet hosts, your terminal type will be set for you automatically
when you first log in. If your terminal type can't be determined automatically, the system may ask you for a terminal type as part of the
login procedure. In any case, if the display is scrambled when you run
gopher, you'll still be able to quit the program by typing Ctrl-C. After
gopher exits, you can change the terminal type. More information on
logging in and setting terminal type can be found in Appendices C
("Logging In") and D ("Just Enough UNIX").

Unlike ftp, telnet, and mail, gopher is not bundled with any commer-
cially available operating system or network software. Consequently,

there may be no gopher client installed on the computer that provides your Internet access. The surest way to test this on a UNIX system is to issue the gopher command. If you get the message "Command not found," try again, but this time add the path name /usr/local/bin, the directory that most UNIX systems use for locally installed software:

```
/usr/local/bin/gopher
```

If this fails and you get the same message, ask the system administrator if gopher is installed and what the appropriate command is to run a gopher client. If gopher is not installed, you can get a copy from the University of Minnesota via anonymous ftp. If you're working on a UNIX system, you'll need to retrieve the source code for gopher and compile it. Novices shouldn't try to do this without help. If a personal computer provides your point of contact with the Internet, you can retrieve an already compiled client program. See the accompanying sidebar for instructions for retrieving gopher software.

RETRIEVING GOPHER SOFTWARE VIA ANONYMOUS FTP - - - - -

The gopher software is available through anonymous ftp at boombox.micro.umn.edu. Implementations of gopher for various platforms (UNIX, DOS, Windows, Macintosh, NeXT, and others) are kept in subdirectories of /pub/gopher. Each subdirectory contains a README file that explains the directory's contents.

You will find several directories for gopher products for DOS and Windows. The contents of these directories are typically either "self-extracting" archives or archives created with the PKZIP utility (with filenames ending in ".zip"). Both of these file types are binary, so remember to issue the binary command to ftp before you download from these directories.

Once you've retrieved an archive containing one of the gopher products, you'll need to unpack it. For self-extracting archives, you need only execute the file you retrieved. It will unpack itself. Be sure to read the documentation that comes with the program.

The packages in the UNIX subdirectory are in "tar" format, and may be compressed as well. (By convention, archives created with the UNIX tar command have .tar appended to a file name describing the contents and version.) When a tar file is compressed, a .Z extension is added. For example, a file named gopher1.12S.tar.Z is a compressed tar archive of version 1.12 of the gopher software. Both tar files and compressed files are binary: you will need to set the file type to binary if you're using ftp to download files of either type. After downloading this file to your computer, you will need first to decompress it and then to extract the components of the tar archive. Here are the commands to do that:

```
% compress -d gopher1.12S.tar
% tar -xf gopher1.12S.tar
```

The compress command turns the file gopher1.12S.tar.Z into gopher1.12S.tar. The tar command extracts the contents of that file, producing a directory named gopher1.12S. The README file in this directory provides instructions for setting up the gopher configuration and building the software.

If you're unable to install a gopher client on the computer that connects you to the Internet, gopher is also available via telnet. Table 6.2 lists some of these sites and the information needed to connect to them. Telnet to the host nearest you and use the login name for that host from the table. The list of sites that offer telnet access to gopher

table 6.2: Internet Sites with Public Logins to Run Gopher

HOSTNAME	IP ADDRESS	LOGIN	AREA SERVED
consultant.micro.umn.edu	134.84.132.4	gopher	North America
ux1.cso.uiuc.edu	128.174.5.59	gopher	North America
gopher.msu.edu	35.8.2.61	gopher	North America
gopher.ebone.net	192.36.125.2	gopher	Europe
info.anu.edu.au	150.203.84.20	info	Australia
gopher.chalmers.se	129.16.221.40	gopher	Sweden
tolten.puc.cl	146.155.1.16	gopher	South America
ecnet.ec	157.100.45.2	gopher	Ecuador
gan.ncc.go.jp	160.190.10.1	gopher	Japan

clients is subject to change. Consult Yanoff's Internet Services List (Chapter 3 shows how to get there) for sites added recently.

Using gopher

When you run a gopher client and connect to the Mother Gopher at the University of Minnesota, you'll see the menu in Listing 6.2. You can select a menu item by typing its number or you can move the cursor to the desired item with your terminal's arrow keys. Pressing Return will select the item, and the item type will determine what gopher does next. Typing a ? will display a summary of the command that can be executed from a gopher menu. Listing 6.3 shows the gopher help message.

listing 6.2:
The Mother gopher's Root Menu

```
            Internet Gopher Information Client v1.11

            Root gopher server: gopher.tc.umn.edu

  -->   1.  Information About Gopher/
        2.  Computer Information/
        3.  Discussion Groups/
        4.  Fun & Games/
        5.  Internet file server (ftp) sites/
        6.  Libraries/
        7.  News/
        8.  Other Gopher and Information Servers/
        9.  Phone Books/
       10.  Search Gopher Titles at the University of Minnesota <?>
       11.  Search lots of places at the University of Minnesota  <?>
       12.  University of Minnesota Campus Information/




Press ? for Help, q to Quit, u to go up a menu
Page: 1/1
```

listing 6.3:
Gopher Command Help

```
                    Quick Gopher Help
                    -----------------

Moving around Gopherspace
-------------------------
Press return to view a document

Use the Arrow Keys or vi/emacs equivalent to move around

Up ...................: Move to previous line.
Down ................: Move to next line.
```

```
Right Return ........: "Enter"/Display current item.
Left, u  ...........: "Exit" current item/Go up a level.


>, +, Pgdwn, space ..: View next page.
<, -, Pgup, b .......: View previous page.


0-9 ................: Go to a specific line.
m   ................: Go back to the main menu.
```

Bookmarks

```
a : Add current item to the bookmark list.
A : Add current directory/search to bookmark list.
v : View bookmark list.
d : Delete a bookmark/directory entry.
```

Other commands

```
s : Save current item to a file.
D : Download a file.
q : Quit with prompt.
Q : Quit unconditionally.
= : Display Technical information about current item.
O : change options.
/ : Search for an item in the menu.
n : Find next search item.
```

```
The Gopher development team hopes that you find this software useful.
If you find what you think is a bug, please report it to us by sending
e-mail to "gopher@boombox.micro.umn.edu"


Press <RETURN> to continue, <m> to mail, <s> to save, or <p> to print:
```

Most of the time, you will not need any additional information about the items in a gopher menu. However, if you want to see the access information gopher has about an item, position the cursor on that item and press the = key. Listing 6.4 shows what gopher reports when you ask for information about an item. In this example, we asked for information about the first item in the Mother Gopher's Root Menu. Gopher tells us the item's name, its type (type 1 items are directories), the path for getting to the object and a host name and port number that can be used to find the object.

listing 6.4:
Getting Information About a gopher Menu Item

```
Name=Information About Gopher
Type=1
Port=70
Path=1/Information About Gopher
Host=gopher.tc.umn.edu


Press <RETURN> to continue, <m> to mail, <s> to save, or <p> to print:
```

With a terminal-based gopher client, there is usually room for 18 menu items on a single screen, and it is common for gopher to present directory listings that span several screens. In the lower-right corner of the display, gopher shows both the current page and the number of pages for the directory being listed. You can move your view of the listing forward and backward a page at a time with the > and < keys. Notice that moving from page to page in one listing is different from going up to the parent menu (with the u command).

Another tool for searching through multi-page menus is the / command, which searches for a word or string in the names of the menu items in the current listing. Remember that the / command searches for the keyword only in the names of the menu items. Searching the contents of menu items requires an "index Search" menu entry and a full-text index.

TIP

To get a menu of all the gopher servers that are known to the Mother Gopher, select Item 8 (Other Gopher and Information Servers) from the root menu. This selection leads to a menu whose first item is "All the Gopher Servers in the World." When you select this item, the server will return a menu with more than 750 items (about 45 menu screens). The / command comes in handy when browsing this menu.

Creating gopher Menus Ad Hoc

One of the most powerful features of the gopher software is that you can dynamically create new menus that combine items from various other menus. There are three tools that make this possible: *bookmarks, index searches,* and veronica. Gopher's bookmark capability allows you to maintain a list of gopher menus that you visit frequently. At any time during a gopher session, you can retrieve this list and use it as you would any other menu. Bookmarks and information about them are managed by the gopher client program. Veronica is a database that contains the names of menu items in all the gopher servers that can be reached from the University of Minnesota gopher. You query the veronica database from a gopher menu item that prompts you for keywords. Menu item names that contain your keywords are returned to you as a menu. Finally, index searches enable you to query a gopher server for files that contain a keyword you specify. Keyword searches are only possible on files that have been indexed, so you'll have to depend on whoever maintains the files to provide an index and a menu item that allows you to submit queries. Let's look at each of these features in greater detail.

Bookmarks in gopher

Navigating through directories one level at a time using menus is easy but tedious. If there are gopher menus that you use frequently, bookmarks are a way to relieve the tedium. Gopher bookmarks are shortcuts that take you directly to the desired menu or item without winding through all its parent menus.

When you locate a menu item that you know you'll want to visit again, simply position the cursor on that item and type **a** to add the item to your list of bookmarks. To add a bookmark for the current directory, use **A**. Doing this will add access information for the current item to a local file that stores the configuration of your gopher client. (On UNIX systems this file is named .gopherrc.) You can view a list of your bookmarks by typing **v**. Gopher will present the bookmarks to you as a menu, and you can move to any item by simply selecting it. If you want to delete a bookmark from the list, first issue a **v** command to display the list. Position the cursor on the item to be

 ADDING BOOKMARKS BY HAND ― ― ― ― ― ― ― ― ― ― ― ―

When you add a bookmark during a gopher session, you must first maneuver to the item or directory that you're interested in and then use the gopher client's command to add a bookmark. Bookmarks are stored in a section of the .gopherrc file on UNIX systems. On DOS systems look for a file named gopher.rc; Windows systems may store bookmarks in bookmark.ini; the bookmark file for the Macintosh TurboGopher is named BookMark. The TurboGopher's bookmark files are a different format from those used by DOS and UNIX. The file Inside-TurboGopher that accompanies the TurboGopher release explains the format and procedures for handling bookmark files on the Macintosh.

On UNIX and DOS systems, you can add bookmarks manually by editing the gopher configuration files mentioned above. The changes you need to make are not complicated. The .gopherrc file will contain a section labeled "bookmarks," and each bookmark contains the same five fields that are returned by a gopher client's = command. In the .gopherrc file a bookmark will look something like this:

```
bookmarks:
Name=InterNIC Bibliography on the Internet
Host=is.internic.net
Type=0
Port=70
Path=0/infosource/getting-started/bibliography
```

The Name field provides the menu item name that you'll see when you display bookmarks. The Host field contains a fully qualified domain name for the host to which you wish to connect. The Type field describes what type of object this menu item represents. In the example above, Type is set to 0 because the bookmark points to a file. (For the names and identifiers for gopher item types, see Table 6.1.)

Port is the port number needed to connect to the resource the bookmark points to. The example bookmark indicates port 70, the port reserved for gopher servers. The file the bookmark points to can be retrieved via the gopher server on is.internic.net. Path repeats the item identifier (0) and gives the directory path that leads to the file.

deleted and type **d**. Because bookmarks are stored in your local configuration file, they are present whenever you start a gopher session. See the accompanying sidebar for information on adding bookmarks by editing your gopher configuration file.

Veronica: An Index to Gopherspace

Veronica stands for "Very Easy Rodent-Oriented Net-wide Index to Computer Archives." It performs for gopher the same service that archie provides for ftp archives: it is a searchable index of the titles of menu items on gopher servers throughout the Internet. Gopher has become an immensely popular tool for publishing information in the Internet community. However, as more gopher servers have come online, the job of searching through gopher menus to find what you're looking for has become more complicated. Veronica is an application that maintains a database of menu item titles from any gopher server that can be reached from the Mother Gopher at the University of Minnesota. There are veronica databases at a number of different sites, and their contents vary somewhat. You may need to query more than one of these to find the information you're looking for. (See the following sidebar for the location of these databases.)

 LOCATING VERONICA SERVERS – – – – – – – – – – – – – –

Veronica databases can be queried at any of the sites listed below in gopher bookmark format. You can add these entries to your .gopherrc file as bookmarks so you're never more than a menu away from being able to query a veronica database. The availability of veronica servers is one of the items discussed in the veronica FAQ.

University of Nevada at Reno:

```
Name=Search veronica database at UNR
Host=comics.scs.unr.edu
Port=800
Path=
```

The Center for Networked Information Discovery and Retrieval (CNIDR), North Carolina:

```
Name=Search  veronica database at CNIDR
Host=wisteria.cnidr.org
Type=7
Port=2347
Path=
```

NYSERNET, New York:

```
Name=Search veronica database at NYSERNET
Host=nysernet.org
Type=7
Port=2347
Path=
```

Performance Systems International (PSINet), Virginia:

```
Name=Search veronica database at PSINet
Host=gopher.psi.com
Type=7
Port=2347
Path=
```

University of Pisa, Italy:

```
Name=Search veronica database at U. Pisa
Host=serra.unipi.it
Type=7
Port=2347
Path=
```

Veronica databases are queried from a gopher menu. The menu item you select to begin a veronica search has the same icon as other index searches (<?>). Listing 6.5 shows the screen that prompts for keywords in a veronica query. In this example, we're querying the veronica database at the University of Nevada at Reno (UNR). The menu from which we're querying provides access to several different veronica servers and allows you to set the scope of the query. A query of gopherspace will return menu items of any type. You can choose a menu item that only looks for a match in gopher menu items that point to directories. Directory queries generally return faster, but querying all of gopherspace will give you a more detailed picture of what is available. The prompt for keywords reminds you of which type of query you selected. To query for menu item titles that contain the words "small" and "business," you simply type those words and press Return. The results of this query will be displayed as a menu, and the first page of the result menu is shown in Listing 6.6. This query produced enough menu items to require six menu screens. (The first two menu items returned by veronica have long titles that are truncated and don't look like they have anything to do with small business. In fact both are Requests for Proposal (RFPs) that are classified as "Small Business Setasides.")

TIP
- - - - - - -

You can limit the scope of your veronica queries manually by including with your keywords a selector that restricts the query to items of a certain type. The format for this is −t<itemtype> where <itemtype> is the single character identifier for one of gopher's menu item types. (See Table 6.1 above for a list of item types and identifiers.)

listing 6.5:
Searching the veronica Database

```
                Internet Gopher Information Client v1.11

                   Search gopherspace using veronica


      1.   Search gopherspace at NYSERNet <?>
  -->  2.   Search gopherspace at UNR <?>
      3.   Search gopherspace at PSINet <?>
      4.   Search gopherspace at University of Pisa <?>
 +-------------Search gopherspace at UNR-----------------+
 |                                                       |
 | Words to search for  small business                  |
 |                                                       |
 |                  [Cancel ^G] [Accept - Enter]         |
 |                                                       |
 +-------------------------------------------------------+


Press ? for Help, q to Quit, u to go up a menu     Page: 1/1
```

listing 6.6:
Results of a veronica Query

```
                Internet Gopher Information Client v1.11

                  Search gopherspace at UNR: small business

  -->  1.   R4: NCI-CM-27729-72 PRECLINICAL TOXICOLOGY AND PHARMACOLOGY
OF D
      2.   NCI-CM-27729-72 PRECLINICAL TOXICOLOGY AND PHARMACOLOGY OF
DRUG
      3.   At the Small Business Development Center, Academe Gets Down
to Bus
      4.   nsf9318      - NSF 93-18 - Small Business Innovation Research
(SBIR
      5.   sei91414    - 4-14  Small Business Innovation Research
(SBIR) awar
      6.   sei91414.wk1- 4-14  Small Business Innovation Research
(SBIR) awar
      7.   sei91415    - 4-15  Small Business Innovation Research
(SBIR) awar
```

170

8. sei91415.wk1- 4-15 Small Business Innovation Research
(SBIR) awar
        9. DOE Small Business Innovation Research Grants.
        10. Food and Agricultural Sciences Small Business Innovation Res.
        11. DOD ONR Small Business Innovative Research Program.
        12. Digestive Diseases and Nutrition Small Business Innovation R.
        13. Defense Life Sciences Small Business Innovation Research.
        14. Space Life Sciences Small Business Research.
        15. Small Business Development Centers.
        16. Western Virginia Small Business Development Consortium.
        17. Hirshber -- ERIC Review: Enterpreneurship and Small Business
Devel.
        18. Community-Development-and-Small-Business/

Press ? for Help, q to Quit, u to go up a menu
Page: 1/6

Index Searches

Like any other menu-based system, gopher makes your access to information easier by giving you a clear view of your choices at every
step of the way. Often, however, you will have only the names of the
menu items to guide you in making selections from gopher menus,
and you'll have to do a lot of browsing to find what you want. If the group
of files you're interested in has been indexed, you can use the index
to identify files that contain the keywords you specify. Usually you
will be dependent on whoever publishes the files to provide an index.

When you're using the terminal-based gopher client, index
searches appear as menu items with the "<?>" icon. The name of the
menu item usually indicates what files the index covers. After you select an index search item, gopher will prompt you for keywords to be
looked up in the index. When you press Return, the gopher server
will search the index for your keywords and build a menu in which
each item points to a file containing your keywords. If you specify
several keywords, most indexes searchable through gopher will count a
file containing any of the words as a successful match. If nothing in the
index matched your keywords, the result menu will contain an item

saying there were no matches. It may also contain items describing the contents of the index or suggestions for phrasing queries effectively.

Further Into Gopherspace

A little gopher knowledge will go a long way. You've learned the basics of starting a gopher client and probing for information with menus, bookmarks, the veronica database, and index searches. Once you're comfortable with using gopher to find Internet resources, you may find that gopher is the ideal tool for producing an information resource of your own and publishing it for the Internet community. Setting up a gopher server is only slightly more complicated than using a gopher client. To learn about creating gopher servers or to develop more advanced skills using gopher, you'll need some additional documentation.

Documentation on the Internet comes in many forms. There are FAQs (compilations of Frequently Asked Questions) about many topics. FYIs (For Your Information bulletins) and RFCs (Requests for Comment) are generated to inform the Internet community of (and invite commentary about) proposed standards. In the USENET Net News there are open forums about a wide range of topics (Net News is discussed in detail in Chapter 8). Gopher documentation comes in all of these forms. There is a gopher FAQ that is updated periodically. Information about the design of gopher and the gopher protocol can be found in RFC 1436. And gopher is the subject of a USENET newsgroup named comp.infosystems.gopher. (For more information about the RFCs and FYIs, see Appendix B: Internet Documentation.)

These disparate sources of information are collected in a single menu item titled "Information About Gopher" on the Mother Gopher in Minnesota. (This is the first menu item on the Mother Gopher's root menu. The contents of the "Information About Gopher" menu are shown in Listing 6.7. A separate FAQ for veronica is maintained at the University of Nevada at Reno and is available via gopher. Finally, if you're working on a UNIX system that has the gopher client software installed, the first place to look for help is the on-line manual. Type man gopher to see the manual entry for the client program. If the gopher manual pages have not been installed, you'll get the message "No manual entry for gopher."

listing 6.7:
the information about gopher menu

```
Internet Gopher Information Client v1.11

Information About Gopher

-->  1.   About Gopher.
2.   Search Gopher News <?>
3.   Gopher News Archive/
4.   comp.infosystems.gopher (USENET newsgroup)/
5.   Gopher Software Distribution/
6.   Gopher Protocol Information/
7.   University of Minnesota Gopher software licensing
policy.
8.   Frequently Asked Questions about Gopher.
9.   Gopher+ example server/
10. How to get your information into Gopher.
11. New Stuff in Gopher.
12. Reporting Problems or Feedback.
13. big Ann Arbor gopher conference picture.gif <Picture>




Press ? for Help, q to Quit, u to go up a menu
Page: 1/1
```

In the next chapter we'll learn about the World Wide Web, an application that uses hypertext to perform many of the same services as gopher.

HUNTING THROUGH THE INTERNET — — — — — — — — — —

Question   When and where did Hillary Rodham Clinton deliver a speech about women's issues?

Answer   Friday, May 29, 1992 at the Graduation Ceremony for Wellesley College. Connect to the Mother Gopher following this menu path:

```
8.  Other Gopher and Information Servers/
  --> 2.  Search titles in Gopherspace using veronica/
        --> 6.  Search gopherspace using veronica at PSINet <?>
```

When you're prompted for keywords to search for, "clinton" and "women" will find the following items.

```
             Internet Gopher Information Client v1.11
         Search gopherspace using veronica at PSINet: clinton
women

  --> 1.  WOMEN'S ISSUES: Speech (by Hillary Clinton) - 5/29/92.
      2.  WOMEN'S ISSUES: Speech (by Hillary Clinton) - 5/29/92.
```

CHAPTER

7

Browsing the WorldWideWeb

"**H**ey," the electrical engineering major said, "Aren't you what's-his-name, the history major? I haven't seen you since college. What's up?" The bus took the corner as fast as it could and plowed uphill. They grabbed at straps to keep from falling.

- "Oh, right, you're that engineering guy, aren't you?" came the response. "So where's your pocket protector?"

- "They went out of style. Say, do you still keep up with history? I need a good source for info about technology in North America in the 19th century."

- "What on earth for?" the historian asked.

- "Well, I read this book about telegraph operators, and I…"

- "Wait! Internet, right? MIT Telecom Archive? Somebody posted a review of a book about telegraph operators."

- "Well, yeah. How did you know?"

- "I was on the 'net browsing the WorldWideWeb for a reference on optical fiber networks." He waggled an index finger at the engineer. "It leads me to the MIT Telecom archive, and right next to the file I'm looking for there's this review of a book about telegraph operators in the 19th century. 'Whoa,' I say, 'what a trip!' I kind of gave up on history, you know? Yeah, I'm a telecommunications consultant now; I work with cable TV companies trying to move into voice and data networks… It's really weird, you getting into history."

- "No weirder than you trying to be an engineer."

From Trees to Webs

When you use a menu-driven application (such as gopher) to retrieve information, you are guided through the complexities of the Internet in an orderly way. At every step, a menu provides a neat picture of your current location and your choices for further action. Many people find the "tree" metaphor useful for understanding menu-based systems: your search begins at the "root" menu and moves through various levels of branches until you finally arrive at the "leaf" level of the menu tree where you find the information you're after. If the information you retrieve through a menu-based system is incomplete, or if it raises new questions, you'll go back to the root menu and search through the menu tree again looking for something that addresses these new issues. In a conventional menu-based system, every search ends at the leaf level: the files to which the menus lead don't point to other resources that might be useful.

In the Internet community there are visionaries promoting a different way of organizing information. In place of a tree-shaped menu structure, they propose a "web," in which there are as few "dead ends" as possible. In this vision of how information should be structured, even the files and documents you retrieve should be capable of pointing beyond themselves to other useful or related resources. The application that implements this vision on the Internet is the World-WideWeb (W^3).

W^3 was developed at CERN (European Center for Nuclear Research), an institution for high-energy physics research in Geneva, Switzerland. Its original purpose was to promote the sharing of research materials and collaboration between physicists at many different locations. W^3 has developed an eager following outside the High-Energy Physics (HEP) community, and there are more than 100 W^3 servers worldwide. W^3 is very strongly represented in

Europe. CERN has very generously made W^3 available to this larger audience and continues to encourage the proliferation of servers.

W^3 is a client/server application that is similar to gopher in many respects. Like gopher, W^3 lets you retrieve information without having to know where on the Internet that information is stored.

When you first use W^3, it will probably seem a lot like gopher. At every step of the way, you'll have clearly identified choices presented to you in menus. Like gopher, W^3 provides an interface to other Internet applications such as gopher, ftp, WAIS (Wide Area Index Search) or whois. However, W^3 is the only Internet application to catalog resources by subject, and even though the catalog is incomplete, it is a tremendous help in guiding the curious to resources of interest. W^3 is also the only Internet application that is *hypertext-based*. Hypertext is what gives W^3 its web-like character.

The Web and Hypertext

Hypertext is a word first coined in the mid-sixties by Ted Nelson, the free-thinking founder of the Xanadu Project, to describe texts that offer alternatives to sequential reading. Today hypertext has come to signify electronically annotated documents that are linked to other documents (and potentially to graphics or to recorded sounds) that may help interpret or clarify the parent document. Imagine reading something and finding a word whose meaning you don't know. If you're reading plain text, you set it aside and look up the word in a dictionary. If you're reading hypertext, you select the unknown word to find any explanations that are linked to it. The explanation may in turn have links to other documents as well. Pursuing the links from document to document can lead to topics and ideas that might not have occurred to you just from reading the parent document. The trail of hyperlinks isn't limited to documents alone. On a computer that is capable of displaying graphics and playing sounds, the linked-in material need not be text. It could also be a picture or an audio recording. The word "hypermedia" is used to describe such mixed-media presentations.

Creating hypertext is labor-intensive. Ideally every word in a document could have links to other sources of information, and links between documents don't just happen. They are made ("built") using a hypertext editor that encodes text in a language capable of expressing the text's links to other documents. Some documents on W^3 are not hypertext, and even the hypertext documents may not be as heavily linked as you would like. The influence of hypertext is apparent throughout W^3, however. The underlying protocol used by W^3 is the hypertext transfer protocol (HTTP), and the Hypertext Markup Language (HTML) is used to produce and link documents. Working with W^3, you'll see that the distinction between menus and documents or files becomes fuzzy: W^3 menus tend to be wordy because they are actually documents. Documents, because they have links that lead to other resources, begin to take on a menu-like appearance.

Choosing a Browser

The software you use to look at hypertext is called a *browser*. The distinctive characteristic of browsers is that they give you a clear view of where the links are in a hypertext document and a way of following links from one document to another. W^3 browsers are also client programs: they retrieve the documents they display from a server, and of course, the W^3 server must work with browsers in all sorts of display environments. Among W^3 clients, you'll find a line-mode browser, several full-screen browsers, and browsers for graphical user interfaces (GUIs) such as Xwindows, Microsoft Windows, and the Macintosh. See the following sidebar for instructions on locating

W³ browsers you can download from the Internet.

The line-mode browser is the most primitive, but it has the great advantage that you can use it with almost any display terminal and with any kind of connection to the Internet. To start the line-mode browser, log into the host that provides your Internet access, type

---

LOCATING WORLDWIDEWEB BROWSERS – – – – – – – – – –

Browsers for W³ are available via anonymous `ftp` from various sites. CERN has the line-mode browser and a number of GUI browsers for different platforms. Connect to `info.cern.ch` and move to the directory `/pub/www`. The README file in this directory has up-to-date information concerning the software that is available. Already-compiled software can be found under the `bin` directory. This directory has subdirectories for various computer platforms (operating systems or environments). Choose the one you're interested in and `cd` to that directory. For most UNIX platforms you'll find the line-mode browser and the `viola` browser for Xwindows. For Microsoft Windows, you'll find the `Cello` browser. (You can also get the `Cello` browser from Cornell University at `fatty.law.cornell.edu`.) For the Macintosh, you'll find `MacWWW`. Source code for the line-mode browser and some of the other products can be found in `/pub/www/src`.

The `Mosaic` browser for Xwindows-based workstations is available through `ftp.ncsa.uiuc.edu`. After you've connected, `cd` to the `/Web` directory and consult the README file for the Mosaic software.

The `Lynx` full-screen browser is available from the University of Kansas at `ukanaix.cc.ukans.edu`. The directory that contains the software is `/pub/WWW/lynx`. In this directory you'll find the `lynx` browser compiled for several platforms and a compressed `tar` archive of the source code. Compiled versions of the `www`³ full-screen browser can be found at `www.njit.edu` in the `/dist` directory.

www, and press Return. If this results in a "www: Command not found" message, try again using the full pathname: /usr/local/bin/www. If this also returns a "Command not found" message, the line-mode browser is probably not installed on the machine you use for Internet access. If you don't have local access to the line-mode browser, you can telnet to info.cern.ch. (CERN is the home of W^3.) The line-mode browser will start as soon as the telnet connection is made.

Full-screen browsers are a step up. They show you W^3 documents a screen at a time and use the display capability of your terminal (highlighting, reverse video, or underlining) and cursor-movement keys. You can use a full-screen browser over any kind of Internet connection, but if you're working on a UNIX system, you'll have to tell it what kind of terminal you're using. There are several browsers available. The Lynx browser was developed at the University of Kansas, and offers a good selection of features. It allows you to search through the current document for strings. This is particularly useful if the document contains more than a few links. It also supports bookmarks. If you'd like to test the Lynx browser, telnet to ukanaix.cc.ukans.edu and log in as www. Another full-screen browser is www^3. To use this browser, telnet to www.njit.edu and log in as www. Instructions for retrieving these browsers via ftp appear in the sidebar above.

Neither line-mode nor full-screen browsers will be able to display graphics or play sounds for you. For example, W3 can lead you to the catalog for an exhibit of medieval art and historical documents from the Vatican. With a line-mode browser, you can read the modern commentary from the catalog, but with a GUI browser, you'll be able to see the pictures and view facsimiles of the documents from the comfort of your own workstation. GUI browsers are also good for looking at several sources at once in different windows. The drawback to GUI browsers is that they have to be run on a machine connected directly to the network. You won't be able to use a GUI browser over a dialup connection unless you have access to SLIP or PPP to extend the Internet protocol to your local machine. Browsers are available for the common GUIs: the Mosaic and Viola browsers for Xwindows, the cello browser for Microsoft Windows, and the Mac_WWW browser for Macintosh.

Using a Browser

When you first start any W^3 client, you'll see the browser's "home page," a page of information that contains links to other documents. The line-mode browser is set up to display the home page shown in Listing 7.1, which was built at CERN.

listing 7.1:
The Home Page for the Line-mode W^3 Browser

```
% www

Overview of the Web
                        GENERAL OVERVIEW
   There is no "top" to the World-Wide Web. You can look at it from
many points of view. If you have no other bias, here are some places
to start:

   by Subject[1]      A classification by subject of
                      interest. Incomplete but easiest to
                      use.

   by Type[2]         Looking by type of service (access
                      protocol, etc) may allow you to find
                      things if you know what you are looking
                      for.

   About WWW[3]       About the World-Wide Web global
                      information sharing project.

Starting somewhere else
```

```
     To use a different default page, perhaps one representing your
field of interest, see   "customizing your home page"[4].

What happened to CERN?

1-6, Up, <RETURN> for more, Quit, or Help: 3
Connection closed by foreign host.
```

In line mode, links to other documents are shown as bracketed numbers following the keyword or phrase to which the link is made. At the bottom of the screen there is a prompt that gives you the range of links from which you can choose (1–6 for the home page shown in Listing 7.1) and a selection of the browser's built-in commands. For help with the browser's commands, type **h** or **help**. The line-mode browser's command set is shown in Table 7.1. All the browser's commands are triggered by pressing Return. (Pressing Return without first entering a command advances the display to the next screenful of the current document.)

With the line-mode browser, to follow any link in the current document you type the number of the link. In Listing 7.1 above, we selected item 3 from the home page to see more information about W^3 itself. This retrieved the page shown in Listing 7.2, which provides a little more information about W^3 itself and a number of pointers to other sources of information. From this page, selecting item 8 brings up the list of Frequently Asked Questions shown in Listing 7.3. In this document, each question points to an answer in a separate document. From the FAQ screen, the Recall command was used to show what documents had been visited so far. The browser could be positioned in any of these documents by typing recall and the number of the item to revisit.

table 7.1: W³ Line-mode Browser Commands

COMMAND	EFFECT
<Return>	Display the next page of the current document.
number	Follow a link (identified by *number*) from the current document and retrieve the document the link points to.
Help	List commands in short form.
Manual	Browse the on-line manual for www. The manual provides more detailed information than the help command.
Back	Go back to the previous document read.
Home	Go back to the first document read.
Recall	List documents you have visited so far. To select one, type "Recall" followed by the number.
List	List the links from the current document by title or, if no title, by pathname. To select a link from this list, type the number by itself as above.
Next, Previous	Go to the next or previous link in the parent document and retrieve that file for browsing.
Go *pathname*	Go to the document represented by the given *pathname*. Pathnames can be relative to the current document or absolute.
Up, Down	Scroll up or down one page in the current document.
Find *keywords*	When an index is available, query it with the supplied keywords. The browser prompt will signal when you can execute find.
Source *command*	Followed by another command (such as print), causes raw source code to be generated for that command. Useful for suppressing interpretation of formatting languages (e.g., PostScript, or W³'s HyperText Markup Language).

table 7.2: W³ Line-mode Browser Commands (continued)

COMMAND	EFFECT
Top, Bottom	Move the browser's view to the top or the bottom of the current document.
Verbose	Toggle verbose mode (for debugging).
Quit	Exit the browser.
Print*	Print the current document, without marking links.
> *file*, >> *file**	Save (or append) the current document in the given file, without marking links.
| *command**	Pipe the current document to the given command, without marking its links.
! command*	Execute the given shell command without leaving www.
CD (or LCD) *directory**	Change directory locally.

*UNIX only

listing 7.2:
Navigating through W³ with the Line-Mode Browser

```
                The World Wide Web project
                    WORLD WIDE WEB

   The WorldWideWeb (W3) is a wide-area hypermedia[1] information re-
trieval initiative aiming to give universal access to a large universe
of documents.

   Everything there is online about W3 is linked directly or indi-
rectly to this document, including an executive summary[2] of the
project, an illustrated talk[3], Mailing lists[4], Policy[5] and Condi-
tions[6], May's W3 news[7], Frequently Asked Questions[8].

   What's out there? [9] Pointers to the world's online information,
subjects[10] , W3 servers[11] , etc.
```

WWW Software Products[12] What there is and how to get it: clients, servers and tools.

Technical[13] Details of protocols, formats, program internals etc

Bibliography[14] Paper documentation on W3 and references. Also: manuals[15] .

1-20, Back, Up, <RETURN> for more, Quit, or Help: **8**

Listing 7.3:
Navigating through W3 with the line-mode browser,
Part 2—Frequently Asked Questions

Frequently Asked Questions on WWW

An FAQ list is really a cop-out from managed information. You should be able to find everything you want to know by browsing from the WWW project page, as everything should be arranged in a logical way. Here though are things which maybe didn't fit into the structure, with pointers to the answers which maybe did. It's an experiment, started May 92. The questioners are anonymous.

I am just starting: how do I find out more?[1]

How does www keep track of the available servers?[2]

How does W3 compare with WAIS and Gopher[3] ?

How do I create my own server[4] ?

Can I get W3 documents if I'm not on the internet[5]?

How can I access WWW through an internet firewall[6]?

See also Nathan Torkington's FAQ list posted every now and again to comp.infosystems.www[7], in hypertext form[8], WWW Primer[9]

Tim BL[10]

1-10, Back, Up, Quit, or Help: **recall**
    Back, Up, <RETURN> for more, Quit, or Help: recall

```
Documents you have visited:-

R  1)   in Overview of the Web
R  2)   in The World Wide Web project
R  3)   in Frequently Asked Questions on WWW

Back, Up, <RETURN> for more, Quit, or Help: quit
```

How Is Not What

As with gopher, how you use the W^3 browser doesn't begin to describe what you can do with W^3. Its capabilities grow as new W^3 servers are added and new documents are published in existing servers. In the early stages of its development, W^3 has lacked a comprehensive index to what is available on its various servers. There is currently no application that does for W^3 what archie does for ftp archives or what veronica does for information on gopher servers. Until there is an application that can give you a reasonable picture of what is available through W^3, you can get oriented by becoming familiar with a few key documents, all of which are easily accessible from the home page.

The W³ Subject Catalog

The first link on the default home page will lead you to the W^3 Subject Catalog. Cataloging Internet resources systematically by subject is something no other Internet application does. (In the tools we've considered so far, only Scott Yanoff's Internet Services List comes close to classifying resources by subject). It is a refreshing change to be able to think about the subject matter you want to investigate instead of guessing at likely names for files that might have something to do with the area of interest. The list of subjects is shown in Listing 7.4. Some of the subject categories are fairly brief ("Fortune Telling," for example); others have so many entries that they are listed separately in another document. Let's look at one of these in detail.

listing 7.4:
The W³ Subject Catalog

The World-Wide Web Virtual Library: Subject Catalogue
WWW VIRTUAL LIBRARY

This is the subject catalogue. See also arrangement by service type[1].
Mail www-request@info.cern.ch to add pointers to this list.

Aeronautics   Mailing list archive index[2]. See also
                     NASA LaRC[3]

Agriculture[4]   Separate list, see also Almanac mail
                     servers[5].

Astronomy and Astrophysics   Abstract Indexes[6] at NASA,
                              Astrophysics work at FNAL[7],
                              Princeton's[8] Sloane Digital
                              Sky Survey, the STELAR[9]
                              project, Space Telescope
                              Electronic Information
                              System[10]. See also: space[11]

Bio Sciences[12]   Separate list.

Computing[13]   Separate list.

Earth Science   US Geological Survey[14].

Education   See the Education Policy Analysis
                     Archives[15] (EPAA), an analysis of
                     education policy at all levels. See also
                     ANU educational materials[16].

Engineering[17]   Separate list.

Environment   HOLIT[18] (Israel Ecological &
                     Environmental Information System), ANU
                     biodiversity services[19], FireNet[20]

Fortune-telling   Tarot Cards[21], I-Ching[22],
                     Biorhythm[23].

```
Geography              World maps[24], CIA World Fact Book[25],
                       India: Miscellaneous information[26],
                       Thai-Yunnan: Davis collection[27], ANU
                       landscape ecology services[28], Manual
                       of Federal Geographic Data Products[29].

History                See Literature & Art[30], Newsgroup,
                       soc.history[31], Soviet Archive[32],
                       1492[33]

Law[34]                US Copyright law[35], Uniform Commercial
                       Code[36], etc, NASDAQ Finance Executive
                       Journal[37].

Libraries[38]          Lists of online catalogues etc.

Literature & Art[39]     separate list.
<Listing truncated>
1-69, Up, <RETURN> for more, Quit, or Help: 39
```

When you select the "Literature & Art" category (39) from the subject catalog, the menu shown in Listing 7.5 appears. Near the bottom is an item labeled as an index to English poetry. Selecting that item, you will see the message displayed in Listing 7.6. Note that the command line prompt now includes the FIND command. To search for poems in this database that contain the word "eclipse," you simply enter that word and press Return. This search will be performed not by W^3, but by WAIS (the Wide Area Information Server), a separate application that specializes in keyword searches of text databases. The query's results (shown in Listing 7.7) have typical WAIS formatting. The numbers at the far left of each line are a relevance score for that entry (1000 is the maximum and indicates a complete match with the keyword). Next are the number of lines in the document that match the keyword, and following this is the citation itself, referring either to the author or to the file containing the poem. Finally, W^3 has appended a link identifier that can be used to retrieve the text of any of the poems.

listing 7.5:
The Literature and Art Catalog

LITERATURE AND ART

Irish Literature   CURIA[1] archive of Irish Literature

English Literature   Project Gutenberg[2]: two classic books
                       a month. See their explanations[3],
                       the index and newsletter[4], books
                       published in 1991[5], 1992[6], and
                       reserved for the USA[7]. See also a new
                       provisional easy-to-use index[8],
                       newsgroup[9] for discussion of the
                       project.

English Literature   The Online Book Initiative[10] is
                       another collection.

Scandinavian Literature   The Runeberg project[11].

Renaissance Culture   Vatican Library Renaissance Culture
                       exhibition[12]

Greek and Latin classics Bryn Mawr Classical Review[13]

Medieval studies   Bryn Mawr Medieval Review[14]

English Poetry   an index[15]

1-20, Back, Up, Quit, or Help: **15**

listing 7.6:
Searching the Poetry Index

POETRY index
                        POETRY

Server created with WAIS release 8 a11 on Fri May 17 15:28:59 1991 by
uriw@microworld
The intention of this server is to collect as many poems as possible.
Right now it contains the complete poems of Shakespeare, Yeats, and
Elizabeth Sawyer, as well as a smattering of many other poets. Read

```
Poetry!

    Specify search words.
    [End]



FIND <keywords>, Back, Up, Quit, or Help: eclipse
```

listing 7.7:
Searching the Poetry Index

- - - - -

```
eclipse (in POETRY)
                        ECLIPSE

   Index POETRY contains the following 5 items relevant to 'eclipse'.
The first figure for each entry is its relative score, the second the
number of lines in the item.

1000   435   TheTower
       /mas/library/Poetry/currently-waised/Yeats/[1]
858    21    Sonnet-107
       /mas/library/Poetry/currently
       -waised/Shakespeare/Sonnets/[2]
858    2139  The_Rape_of_Lucrece
       /mas/library/Poetry/currently-
       waised/Shakespeare/Various_Poems/[3]
858    38    THE SUNNE RISING      John Donne[4]
858    312   Ezra Pound     (bio by Bill Gilson)[5]


    [End]


FIND <keywords>, 1-5, Back, Up, Quit, or Help:
```

This search is typical of the versatility of W^3. Browsing through subjects, you should not have to be concerned over which application manages the information you want or what type of file the information is stored in. Whether or not the resource is within W^3 and whether or not it is hypertext, W^3 will provide an interface using its conventions for hypertext links.

W³ Gateways to Internet Services

The home page entry that leads to resources by type is a W^3 gateway to other Internet applications. (This page appears in Listing 7.8.) From this one page in W^3 you can branch to approximately two dozen Internet applications or sources of information. Some of these services (archie, ftp, gopher, telnet, Yanoff's list) will be familiar to you; others (Art St. George's list, WAIS, X.500, for example) may still be unknown. You can get to them all from this menu. When you use W^3 as a gateway to other applications, the user interface will resemble W^3's.

listing 7.8:
Internet Services Accessible from W³

```
                    Data sources classified by access protocol
                    DATA SOURCES CLASSIFIED BY TYPE OF SERVICE

            See also categorization by subject[1].

    World-Wide Web[2]      List of W3 native "HTTP" servers. These
                           are generally the most friendly. See
                           also: about the WWW initiative[3].

    WAIS[4]                Find WAIS index servers using the
                           directory of servers[5], or lists by
                           name[6] or domain[7]. See also: about
                           WAIS[8].

    Network News[9]        Available directly in all www browsers.
                           See also this list of FAQs[10].

    Gopher[11]             Campus-wide information systems, etc,
                           listed geographically. See also: about
                           Gopher[12].

    Telnet access[13]      Hypertext catalogues by Peter Scott.
                           See also: list by Scott Yanoff[14].
                           Also, Art St George's index[15] (yet to
                           be hyperized), etc.
```

```
VAX/VMS HELP[16]      Available using the help gateway[17] to
                      WWW.

Anonymous FTP[18]     Tom Czarnik's list of (almost) all sites.
                      Search them all with full hypertext
                      archie gateways[19] (or telnet to
                      ARCHIE[20])-- An index of almost
                      everything available by anonymous FTP.

TechInfo[21]          A CWIS system from MIT. Gateway access
                      thanks to Linda Murphy/Upenn. See also
                      more about techninfo[22].


X.500[23]             Directory system originally for
                      electronic mail addresses. (Slightly
                      uneven view though gateway).

  WHOIS[24]           A simple internet phonebook system.

Other protocols       Other forms of online data[25].

Tim BL[26]

    [End]
1-26, Back, Up, Quit, or Help: 2
```

The W³ Gateway to archie and ftp

In Chapter 3 we discussed the use of archie and ftp. You can also use W^3 to perform archie queries and retrieve files via ftp. From the "By Type" document, selecting the "full hypertext archie gateway," item 19, leads to the menu shown in Listing 7.9. From this screen you can select any of several kinds of archie query and specify the keywords to be used in searching the archie database. W^3 provides a choice of archie hypertext servers for you to use. There are differences in the databases at these sites, and if your query against one of these databases returns no results, you should submit it to the other server. In this example the keyword "telephony" is entered. The results of the query are displayed as a page of hypertext that provides a link to the filename that matched the keyword, a link to the directory that contains that file, and a link to the site that maintains the ftp archive in which this file was found. Selecting any of these links will open an ftp session to the host selected. Selecting the file link retrieves the file and displays it on your screen. Selecting the directory link provides a menu of all the files in that directory. Selecting the host link opens an ftp session starting at the topmost ftp directory on that host.

listing 7.9:
Archie and Anonymous ftp via W³

```
Hypertext Archie Servers
                    [1]HYPERTEXT ARCHIE SERVERS

   This is a list of full-hypertext archie servers around the world.
If you know any that are not on the list please let me know.

     ArchiePlex at NEXOR[2].

     Warchie at Nottingham CRG (UK)[3]
```

```
Martijn Koster[4]

     [End]

1-4, Back, Quit, or Help: 2

         ARCHIEPLEX CASE INSENSITIVE SUBSTRING SEARCH

   ArchiePlex locates files available for anonymous FTP. This service
uses the Archie server at archie.sura.net to execute the searches. For
more information see ArchiePlex info[1].

   Please specify a search term.

   See also:

     This search sorted by Date[2]

     ArchiePlex Substring Search[3]
```

```
      ArchiePlex Exact Search[4]
```

```
Martijn Koster[5]

FIND <keywords>, 1-5, Back, Up, Quit, or Help: telephony

   RESULT FOR ARCHIEPLEX CASE INSENSITIVE SUBSTRING SEARCH

   These are the results found for the ArchiePlex Case Insensitive Sub-
string Search[1] for telephony

cs.dal.ca[2]

      windows-telephony-specs-available-in-postscript[3] 2K (15-05-93)
in /comp.archives/comp.dcom.modems/[4]

nctucca.edu.tw[5]

      tech.telephony.gz[6] 610 bytes (17-02-92) in
      /USENET/news.announce.newgroups/tech/[7]
```

```
Martijn Koster[8]

      [End]
1-8, Back, Quit, or Help: 3
```

The W³ Index to FAQs of All Sorts

FAQs (compilations of Frequently Asked Questions) are an Internet institution. FAQ documents exist for hundreds of topics discussed on the Internet. FAQs are a very helpful form of documentation if you can find them. Many FAQs are posted to USENET newsgroups regularly, but finding the right newsgroup can sometimes be difficult. W³ simplifies this dramatically by collecting links to more than 300 FAQs (about all sorts of topics) in a single hypertext document. Retrieving an FAQ requires only that you select a link from this list. The list of FAQs is an item in the "Network News" portion of the menu that lists services By Type.

All the W³ Servers in the World and Their Home Pages

Finally, if you want to get an overview of the world of W^3 servers, W^3 itself is one of the resources in the classification of services by type. When you select item 2 from the Services By Type document, a menu of available W^3 servers will be displayed. (A portion of this menu is shown in Listing 7.10.) You can connect to any of the servers listed by simply selecting its link from this document. From the list of W^3 servers there is a link to an automatically collected list of "home pages" for various servers. (The title for this document refers to "HTTP" servers. HTTP is the hypertext transfer protocol used by W^3.) This is a particularly useful list if you are working with either a full-screen or a GUI browser that supports bookmarks. (The line-mode browser does not.)

listing 7.10:
The List of World Wide Web Servers

```
World-Wide Web Servers

                        W3 SERVERS

    This is a list of registered WWW[1] servers alphabetically by conti-
nent, then by country. There are also many unregistered servers. Note
that one server machine can serve many databases. See also: data avail-
able by other protocols[2], data by subject[3], how to make a new
server[4], test servers[5], automatically collected list[6] of Home
Pages. If servers are marked "experimental", you should not expect any-
thing. Please send announcements of new servers to
www-request@info.cern.ch.


Europe (including Scandinavia)

EXUG[7]                 The European X User Group

AUSTRIA

SIGGRAPH[8]             ACM SIGGRAPH Bibliography of
                        references on Graphics in
                        computing. Gatewayed From Hyper-G
```

```
Technical University of Graz[9]
                    Information service. Gateway to
                    Hyper-G data.
1-168, Back, Up, <RETURN> for more, Quit, or Help: 6
```

The Appeal of the Web

W^3 is an attractive application for many audiences. For new users of the Internet it provides a uniform interface for network applications and a subject catalog that eases the task of finding resources. For experienced users it provides an open-ended technological playground that can take advantage of multimedia extensions of workstation hardware. The absence of a comprehensive index along the lines of archie or veronica makes W^3 less usable than it might be, but as the number of servers grows, indexing their contents will become a higher priority.

HUNTING THROUGH THE INTERNET

Question 1   What is the Crocodile's Dilemma?

Answer   From the WWW line-mode browser's default home page, choose "By Subject." The Mathematics section of the Subject Catalog has an entry for Paradoxes (link 50 as of this writing, but the number will change if the top portion of the list has items added or restructured). Selecting Paradoxes produces a menu with Crocodile's Dilemma as an entry. When you select that item, you'll read the following story (courtesy of Tom Georges with commentary by Daryl Barber):

```
                    CROCODILE'S DILEMMA
     A crocodile[1] seized a human baby who had been playing on the
banks of the Nile. The mother implored the crocodile to return her
child. "Well," said the crocodile, "if you can predict accurately
what I will do then I will return your child. However, if you guess
wrong, I will eat it for my lunch."
```

```
    "Oh, you will devour my baby!!" cried the distraught mother.
    "Now," said the wily crocodile, "I cannot return your baby, for
if I do return it, I shall make you speak falsely and I warned you
that if you spoke falsely I would devour it."
    "Quite the contrary," said the clever mother, "you cannot devour
my baby, for if you do devour it, you will make me speak the truth
and you promised me that if I spoke truly, you would return my
baby. I know you are an honorable crocodile and one who will keep
his word."
Who is right??
 Please feel free to annotate this document.
1-3, Back, <RETURN> for more, Quit, or Help:
```

Question 2 What was the original form of Murphy's Law? Who first stated it and when?

Answer Connect to the Mother Gopher and select Item 8 ("Other Gopher and Information Servers") from the root menu. From this menu select item 2, "Search titles in Gopherspace using `veronica`." That selection will bring up a menu of sites with `veronica` databases. Pick one and query for "murphy law." This will return a single menu page of titles that match. (Note that querying for the word "murphy" alone will return many more titles.) The resulting menu contains an entry titled "Murphy's Law," which provides the following information:

```
Murphy's Law: prov. The correct, *original* Murphy's Law reads: "If
there are two or more ways to do something, and one of those ways can
result in a catastrophe, then someone will do it."
<--Entry Truncated-->
Edward A. Murphy, Jr. was one of the engineers on the rocket-sled
experiments that were done by the U.S. Air Force in 1949 to test hu-
man acceleration tolerances (USAF project MX981). One experiment in-
volved a set of 16 accelerometers mounted to different parts of the
subject's body. There were two ways each sensor could be glued to
its mount, and somebody methodically installed all 16 the wrong way
around. Murphy then made the original form of his pronouncement,
which the test subject (Major John Paul Stapp) quoted at a news con-
ference a few days later.
```

The USENET Bazaar

"In downtown Cleveland today, Elvis was sighted on a municipal bus. Stunned onlookers reported that the former king of rock and roll sat quietly at the back of the bus working on a crossword puzzle and whistling 'My Way.'

"In other news, Silicon Valley chip makers announced plans to build a 64-unit multithreaded vector superprocessor with hardware support for asynchronous task generation. Prototype units, expected in early 1996, will also feature bidirectional optical waveguides and wormhole routing for virtual cut-through communications.

- "On the local front, rosebody@wsqpd.com pitched a hissy fit over the deluge of recent items in this broadcast concerning the changing of light bulbs. To quote rosebody: 'This is just great. First, we had the anecdote, then we had someone quoting the **whole tedious anecdote** just to add two lines, and now someone else has quoted the quote and included the original, **and** accidentally failed to add anything new at all. I can't stand it.'

- "Thanks for sharing that, rosebody!

- "This just in: worms in hostage food! Details at 11:00.

- "New FAQs were posted to news.answers today from soc.culture.hongkong, comp.lsi.cad, and comp.lang.modula2.

- "From the weather desk in Chicago: tropical storm Emily now off the coast of Newfoundland is rapidly losing tropical characteristics.

- "And in news.groups, heated debate continues over the proposed formation of a soc.culture.tibet newsgroup.

- "That's it for tonight's broadcast. In the words of Scoop Nisker, 'If you don't like the news, go out and make some of your own.' Good night and have a pleasant tomorrow."

The Biggest Bulletin Board in the World

In 1979 students at Duke University and the University of North Carolina constructed a system of UNIX shell scripts to move messages between two computers using the UUCP (UNIX-to-UNIX Copy) protocol over phone lines. (UUCP is a protocol used by UNIX systems to transfer files automatically. One system calls another at a pre-arranged time. The calling computer logs in to a special user account that runs the file transfer program.) The messages that moved between Duke and UNC made up a floating bulletin board, a copy of which resided at each site. Discussions in this system were organized by topic, and when a reader of a topic at one site contributed something new to a discussion, that response would be distributed to all the copies of the bulletin board. The participating computers contacted each other regularly to exchange new topics and responses to topics.

This system went on to become the USENET News, or simply Net News. Net News developed in the UNIX community, initially with no ties to the Internet. Until the mid-1980s, the USENET newsgroups were circulated primarily via UUCP. But more and more of the USENET sites were also Internet hosts, and in 1986, after two years of development, the Network News Transfer Protocol (NNTP) was introduced to the Internet community at large as a tool for distributing Net News. The already popular Network News was projected to an Internet-wide audience. NNTP dramatically increased the efficiency of transferring Net News articles from site to site, and it made the news available through client/server applications. Client/server access brought the Network News to people who did not have a local copy of the newsgroups. As the Internet has grown, so has USENET. Today there are more than 4000 newsgroups that are distributed via NNTP.

Net News is arguably the world's most comprehensive bulletin board. In spite of the symbiotic relationship between USENET and the Internet, they are not the same thing. There are, for example, sites that still depend on UUCP to exchange news with the USENET and Internet communities, and simply being on the Internet does not guarantee a News feed. Whether or not your local point of contact with the Internet has its own copy of the USENET newsgroups, however, you should be able to read the Net News from almost any Internet host.

Tools for Reading the News

To read the Network News, you need access to an Internet host that carries Net News and a news reader. A news reader is a program that manages your subscriptions to newsgroups. It keeps track of what groups you're interested in and what articles you've already read in those groups. As new articles are posted to the newsgroups you follow, the news reader lets you read and respond to these postings. Before the development of NNTP, news readers were conventional, stand-alone programs, and could only be used on computers that had local access to the text of the newsgroups. NNTP fostered the development of news readers as client programs that could be used anywhere on a local network to read the news from a central location. You'll find news readers of both types in use throughout the Internet.

Most sites that provide Net News access maintain several of the popular readers as well. Readnews is a line-mode reader that is widely distributed, but not well-suited to reading a large number of newsgroups. Its main advantages are that it is in wide distribution, has a command set that is easy to learn, and can be run on almost any terminal available. Vnews, rn and nn are newer, screen-oriented news readers that are also available at many sites. The ability to scroll through a list of newsgroups is a distinct advantage over line-mode readers. Fancier still are the `trn` and `tin` readers. These, too, are screen oriented, but they offer the added benefit of organizing news articles into conversational *threads*. Each thread contains an original article and all responses to that article. Packaging articles and responses together makes for easier reading and cuts down on redundant and misinformed responses. There are also news readers for various GUI Systems (Xwindows, MS Windows, and Macintosh).

You can get information about further developments in news reader software from the USENET itself in the group `news.software.readers`. Here you'll find plenty of discussion about news reader features, and you're likely to find an article by Gene Spafford that gives a detailed view of the history of Net News software development. This article is also posted to `news.answers` and `news.announce.newusers`, and is available via anonymous `ftp` in the pub/usenet/news.answers/usenet-software directory at pit-manager.mit.edu. Many of the news readers now in circulation are available via anonymous `ftp`. Consult your system administrator before attempting to install a news reader; it's not something a new user should undertake unassisted.

In the examples below we'll use the `tin` reader because it has an easy-to-read display and shows off threads nicely. (Just in case it's not obvious, we're also using entirely fictitious newsgroups.) Tin is a particularly good news reader for new users. It has a relatively simple command set, its help screens are uncluttered, and the documentation for `tin` is succinct and written clearly. There are more popular news readers, but `tin` is widely distributed and easy to use.

Reading the News

Starting a news reader is just like executing any other command: just type the name of your news reader and press Return. A first-time user starting the tin news reader on an Internet host will see a screen like the one shown in Listing 8.1. Some versions of tin may precede this Group Selection screen with a page of instructions and command help.

listing 8.1:
The Initial Screen for the Tin News Reader

```
                    Group Selection (4722)      h=help

--> u 1      - control
    u  2      - test
    u  3      - junk
    u  4      - to.wsqpd
    u  5      - to.wsqpdsv
    u  6      - wsqpd.announce
    u  7      - wsqpd.general
    u  8      - wsqpd.games
    u  9      - wsqpd.internet
    u 10      - wsqpd.mail
    u 11      - wsqpd.modems
    u 12      - wsqpd.netnews
    u 13      - wsqpd.netnews.stats
    u 14      - wsqpd.software
    u 15      - wsqpd.software.amiga
    u 16      - wsqpd.software.atari.st

    <n>=set current to n, TAB=next unread, /=search pattern,
c)atchup,  g)oto, j=line down, k=line up, h)elp, m)ove, q)uit, r=tog-
gle all/unread, s)ubscribe, S)ub pattern, u)nsubscribe, U)nsub
pattern, y)ank in/out
```

Tin has a structured approach to news reading. You first select a newsgroup, then choose threads to read within that group, and finally read the postings in the chosen thread. The first screen tin shows is "Group Selection." From this screen you can scroll through the newsgroups that are active at your site. (The news administrator at a site chooses which newsgroups the site will carry. A site does not have to accept all the newsgroups that are offered to it.) The number following the screen title is the number of newsgroups your site has available. The center portion of the Group Selection screen is a window showing 16 newsgroups. At the left edge of the screen is a single-letter status indicator. In this case, none of the groups has been read previously ("u" indicates unread). Following the status indicator is a selection number. After your first session of reading news, the selection number will be followed by the number of articles currently posted to the news group. The number of articles is based on new postings since the last time news was read. If you're reading news for the very first time, a dash will be substituted for the number of articles (as in Listing 8.1). Following the numbers is the name of the group.

Tin includes a help message at the bottom of the screen describing the key commands that can be executed from the current screen. (The on-screen help can be toggled on and off with the H command.) In the Group Selection screen there are commands to manage your subscription to news groups and commands to move around in the list of available groups. Type h for a complete list of tin commands.

Subscribing, Unsubscribing, and Catching Up

When you first read Net News, you'll be presented with a list of all the active newsgroups as though they are all of equal interest. Even a broad-minded person with renaissance proclivities, however, will become more selective when faced with 4722 newsgroups. You can make your newsgroup reading more enjoyable by establishing a subscription list tailored to your interests. Most news readers offer commands to subscribe to and unsubscribe from groups.

Tin's subscription management commands can be applied to individual newsgroups or to collections of newsgroups. For individual newsgroups you simply position the current group pointer on a group in your list and issue the subscribe (s) or unsubscribe (u) command. You can also apply a subscription command to any collection of newsgroups whose names share a common pattern; use S to subscribe and U to unsubscribe. After you've entered the command, you'll be prompted for a pattern or keyword that identifies the collection of groups.

Even after you've created a subscription list that reflects your interests, you may not always want to read every posting in a group. If you leave too many things unread, finding new postings can be a chore. The "catch-up" command (c) helps you cope with this by marking everything in a newsgroup as read. After you use the catch-up command, you'll see only new postings for the newsgroup.

Newsgroup Navigation

By default, tin uses reverse video to mark your current position in the newsgroup and article lists. Tin can be configured to use an arrow (-->) instead, and we'll use this indicator for clarity's sake. (You can display all the configurable features of tin with the M command.) The highlighted group can be selected at any time by pressing Return. There are three ways to move around in the list of newsgroups that the group selection screen presents:

- Use control characters to scroll forward (Ctrl-F) and backward (Ctrl-B) in the list of active news groups.

- Move to a specific group by typing its number. The group you jump to need not be on the current screen. The display will reposition to the group whose number you type.

■ Search the newsgroup list for a word or pattern (the / key searches forward, ? searches backward.)

Searching the titles of the newsgroups is a particularly helpful feature. To find newsgroups about Elvis, for example, you would simply type /elvis and press Return. The current group pointer will move to the first group whose name contains the word "elvis," as shown in Listing 8.2. This search will find the group alt.elvis.sighting, which currently has 28 postings. By pressing Return you can display the contents of this newsgroup.

listing 8.2:
finding Newsgroups about Elvis

```
                    Group Selection (4722)              h=help

      2497 370   fj.windows.ms
      2498 1451  fj.rec.motorcycles
      2499 161   de.alt.bbs.waffle
      2500 369   su.computers.mac
      2501 88    su.computers.ibm
      2502 101   su.computers.unix
      2503 83    su.computers.next
      2504 22    su.computers.amiga
      2505       biz.digex.announce
      2506 184   austin.music
      2507 3027  news.admin.misc
      2508 4945  news.admin.policy
      2509 155   news.admin.technical
-->   2510 28    alt.elvis.sighting
      2511 1     alt.casting.porosity
      2512 111   alt.peace.corps

      <n>=set current to n, TAB=next unread, /=search pattern,
c)atchup, g)oto, j=line down, k=line up, h)elp, m)ove, q)uit, r=toggle
all/unread, s)ubscribe, S)ub pattern, u)nsubscribe, U)nsub pattern,
y)ank in/out
```

After you select a group, tin will give you an overview of the contents of the group as a series of threads or conversations. Like the group selection screen, the overview of threads in a newsgroup is organized into a menu. Listing 8.3 shows the overview of threads in the group alt.elvis.sighting. The name of the current group appears at the top of the screen followed by the number of threads and the number of articles in the group. The threads are numbered sequentially and you can navigate through them with the same commands as in the Group Selection menu. The plus sign indicates that the thread contains articles you have not yet read. The second number in each thread entry is the number of articles in that thread, and the last field contains the subject line for the thread.

When you're looking at the contents of a newsgroup, even in summary form, you have several options that were not available at the Group Selection Menu. A summary of these commands appears in the screen shown in Listing 8.3. You can list the contents of each thread by author and date posted with the l command.

listing 8.3:
Overview of articles posted to alt.elvis.sighting

```
                alt.elvis.sighting (17T 32A)            h=help

-->  1 + 7 ELVIS IS BARNEY!
     2 +     Contest Announcement!
     3 + 2 Elvis seen in Maine
     4 +     ELVIS STAMPS-strange happenings????
     5 + 2 elvis is dead
     6 +     test
     7 +     elvis at Barnes & noble
     8 +     Elvis and the like
     9 +     I seen him
    10 + 1 Brent's Massive USENET Crossposting Onslaught From Hell.
```

```
11 + innocence
12 + 1 I Didn't See Elvis
13 + <None>
14 + worked with elvis
15 + 2 Stop it just stop it!
16 + Elvis and me...

<n>=set current to n, TAB=next unread, /=search pattern, ^K)ill/se-
lect, a)uthor search, c)atchup, j=line down, k=line up, K=mark read,
l)ist thread, l=pipe, m)ail, o=print, q)uit, r=toggle all/unread,
s)ave, t)ag, w=post
```

When you select any of the threads from this menu, `tin` will bring up the text of the posted article. When you've finished reading the first article, you'll have the option of moving to the next article in the thread, moving to the next thread, or returning to the overview of threads and articles.

Reading and Responding to Articles

The text of Net News articles looks a lot like an e-mail message. Listing 8.4 shows a message from the `alt.casting.porosity` newsgroup. At the top of the screen `tin` provides information about the current newsgroup, which thread you're reading, and the number of responses. The slogan about passwords at the end of the message is the "signature" of the user who posted the article. A signature is a message that is automatically appended to a user's postings. (Each user's signature is kept in a file named `.signature` in the user's home directory. If you post to newsgroups from your workplace, it's a good idea to put a disclaimer in your signature file to remind your audience that you're speaking on your own authority and not that of your employer.)

listing 8.4:
Reading a News Article with tin

```
Mon, 06 Sep 1993 11:47:50          alt.casting.porosity
Thread 1 of 1
Article 443926                              Casting Porosity FAQ?
     No responses
bkf@optimism.wsqpd.com                 Bennett Falk at W.S.Q.P.&D.

When will the new version of the Casting Porosity FAQ be posted?

Bennett
-----
Passwords are like underwear,
both should be changed often.

bkf@optimism.wsqpd.com


 <n>=set current to n, TAB=next unread, /=search pattern, ^K)ill/se-
lect, a)uthor search, c)atchup, f)ollowup, j=line down, k=line up,
K=mark read, l=pipe, m)ail, o=print, q)uit, r)eply mail, s)ave, t)ag,
w=post

                          -- Last response --
```

After you've read an article, you can save it in a file, send it to the printer, mail it to someone, send it as input to another program, or tag it as part of a collection of articles you'll work with later. Commands similar to those offered by tin are available in most other news readers as well.

If you're moved to respond to the article you've just read, you can either send a reply to the author via e-mail or post a follow-up response to the newsgroup, depending on the audience you want to reach. Replies sent to the author go directly to that person's mailbox and will probably come to his or her attention before follow-up postings in the newsgroup. E-mail replies don't become part of the newsgroup. If the point you want to make is of general interest to readers of the newsgroup, post it as a follow-up response.

When you respond via e-mail or with a follow-up article, your news reader will create a header for the response and start an editor for you to compose the message to be sent to the author or posted to the newsgroup. Tin uses the vi editor by default, but you can override this choice by setting the environment variable VISUAL to the full pathname (e.g., /usr/ucb/ex) for a different editor. (For more information on pathnames and setting environment variables in UNIX, see Appendix D.) In Listing 8.5, the UNIX vi editor is used to edit a follow-up response. (The lines beginning with the "~" character indicate that the message being edited is shorter than vi's screen.)

The vi editor is a complex piece of software in its own right; however, you only need to know a couple of commands to use it for brief messages. When vi first starts, it puts you in "cursor movement" mode. You can move the cursor around using four keys: h (left), j (down), k (up), and l (right). When the cursor is positioned where you want to enter text, you can enter "insert" mode by typing i. In insert mode anything you type will be inserted into the document. Vi does not break lines automatically. You'll have to press Return at the end of each line. While you're in insert mode, you can backspace over characters, but vi's cursor movement commands won't work. When you're finished entering text, press the Escape key. This turns off insert mode and returns you to "cursor movement" mode. When you're through editing, press Escape to set the editor to cursor movement mode. To save your work and quit the editor, first enter command mode by typing a colon(:). The colon will be displayed on the bottom line of the screen. Next type wq and press Return to write your changes and quit the editor. (If you just want to exit the editor, type q! instead of wq.).

listing 8.5:
Editing a Follow-up Response in vi

```
Newsgroups: alt.casting.porosity
References: <1993Sep6.184750.18152@optimism.wsqpd.com>
Organization: WSQPD
Distribution: usa

Bennett (bkf@wsqpd.com) wrote:
: When will the new version of the Casting Porosity FAQ be posted?

: Bennett
: --
: Passwords are like underwear,
: both should be changed often.
:
: bkf@optimism.wsqpd.com

No changes to the casting porosity faq have been received in the last
six weeks, so there won't be a new edition for at least another month.
Readers of this newsgroup are encouraged to contribute suggestions and
articles for the FAQ. New postings should occur on the 15th of each
month.

Thanks,
rosebody
~
~
~
~
~
~
:wq
q)uit, e)dit, i)spell, p)ost: p
```

The procedure for posting an entirely new article to a newsgroup
is very similar to that for posting a follow-up response. In the tin
news reader, the w command is used to post a new article to the current newsgroup. Tin creates a template header for the new article and
starts the editor for you. From this point on, the procedure is exactly
like posting a follow-up response.

Depending on the news reader you use and the group you post to, you may have the opportunity to specify how widely distributed your article should be. The default distribution for new articles in the core USENET newsgroups is worldwide. (The core categories for USENET newsgroups will be discussed in detail shortly.) Your news reader may give you a choice of distributions that let you target your posting for the area to which it is relevant. The distribution choices will vary considerably from site to site, but common distributions are:

world	Worldwide Distribution (default)
can	Canada
eunet	European sites in EUNet
na	North America
usa	United States

You will probably have local or regional distribution categories available as well. Many states have distribution categories (ca for California, ga for Georgia, and so on).

The Taxonomy of Newsgroups

When you read Net News, you'll see scores of discussion groups, each consisting of articles posted by the people interested in the group's topic. As you've seen from the examples above, most USENET newsgroups have brief descriptive names that let the potential reader know what topic is under discussion. With 4000-plus newsgroups in circulation, finding topics you're interested in can be difficult no matter how well-named they are.

One way of making the newsgroups more manageable is to classify them into very general areas of interest, and that classification produces names in the format shown above. In any newsgroup name the leftmost word (comp, misc, rec, soc, alt, etc.) indicates a general category for the discussion. The rest of the newsgroup name is not as orderly, but by convention, the words in a newsgroup name represent more specific spheres of interest as you read from left to right. For example, groups dealing with computer-related issues begin with comp. The comp groups that discuss artificial intelligence add .ai, and there are groups named comp.ai, comp.ai.edu, comp.ai.philosophy, comp.ai.shells, and comp.ai.vision.

Categories of USENET Newsgroups

At the most general level, there are seven categories for official USENET newsgroups. Newsgroups in these categories are distributed worldwide to all USENET sites. A local administrator may elect not to carry groups in these core categories, but everything in these categories is offered to each USENET site. These global newsgroup categories don't change often, but they do change, and new newsgroups are added to each category nearly every day. Changes to these categories and a classification of the currently active newsgroups are posted periodically in "news.groups." (See Table 8.1 for a brief description of the globally distributed groups.)

table 8.1: Global USENET Newsgroups

CATEGORY	DESCRIPTION
comp	Newsgroups dealing with computer-related topics including hardware, software, commercial applications, and distribution of public domain and shareware programs.
misc	Newsgroups that cut across categories or that address themes not easily classified under any of the other groups.
news	Discussions related to Net News distribution and software.

table 8.1: Global USENET Newsgroups (continued)

CATEGORY	DESCRIPTION
rec	Groups discussing recreational activities, the arts and other enjoyable things.
sci	Discussions related to topics in the sciences.
soc	Discussion groups for social issues.
talk	Groups providing an opportunity for open-ended debate.

Where New Newsgroups Come From

Starting a new topic in one of these core categories begins with submitting a proposal to the group news.announce.newgroups and to any newsgroups related to the proposed new topic. Submitting the proposal begins a period of discussion in which the charter and the name of the proposed new group are defined. At the end of the discussion period (usually 30 days), if the proposal is generally received favorably and if the name and charter have been agreed upon, a vote is taken via e-mail. Interested parties have 21 to 31 days to express an opinion about the formation of the new group. To be approved, the new group must be approved by at least two-thirds of the votes cast and must receive at least 100 more affirmative votes than negative votes.

The Alternative Newsgroup Hierarchy

In addition to the core USENET News categories there are a number of alternative newsgroup classifications. Groups in these categories are distributed locally by agreement between sites. The newsgroups in these alternative categories are technically not part of the USENET News even though they are distributed via the same channels and read with the same news readers. The alternative groups are not governed by the same evaluation process as the USENET groups. Because the alternative groups are distributed by local agreement, they may not be as widely circulated as the core USENET groups. When you read the Network News, however, the USENET groups and the alternative groups will show up side by side. A list of the categories for alternative groups appears in Table 8.2.

table 8.2: Categories for Alternative Newsgroups

CATEGORY	DESCRIPTION
alt	A collection of "alternative" newsgroups distributed voluntarily by a collection of sites. Many Usenet sites do not receive these groups.
bionet	Newsgroups for topics of interest to biologists, originating from net.bio.net.
bit	Newsgroups redistributing discussions from popular BitNet LISTSERV mailing lists.
biz	Newsgroups concerned with business products, particularly computer products and services. Postings include product reviews and announcements of product releases, bug fixes, and enhancements.
clarinet	Newsgroups publishing material from commercial news services and other sources. Sites carrying the ClariNet groups pay a licensing fee for the groups.
gnu	Newsgroups connected with Internet mailing lists of the GNU Project of the Free Software Foundation.
hepnet	Discussions dealing with High Energy Physics and Nuclear Physics. These groups, too, are connected to mailing lists and automatically archived.
ieee	Newsgroups related to the Institute of Electrical and Electronics Engineers (IEEE).

table 8.2: Categories for Alternative Newsgroups (continued)

CATEGORY	DESCRIPTION
Inet/DDN	Discussions, many affiliated with Internet mailing lists. Groups in this category do not have a unique category name.
Info	A diverse collection of mailing lists (many technical, some cultural and social) connected into news at the University of Illinois.
k12	Conferences concerned with K-12 education: curriculum, language exchanges, and classroom-to-classroom projects.
relcom	A hierarchy of Russian-language newsgroups distributed mostly on the territory of the former Soviet Union (non-CIS countries included). These groups are available in Europe and Northern America; because of the 8-bit encoding (KOI-8) of Cyrillic letters, minor software modifications may be required.
u3b	Groups dealing with AT&T 3B series computers.
vmsnet	Topics for VAX/VMS users. Maintenance of these groups is a project of the VMSnet work group of the VAX SIG of the US Chapter of DECUS (the Digital Equipment Computer User's Society).

The Human Dimension

The Network News is a source of information unlike any other. Nowhere on the Internet is it more apparent that information is something made by human beings. When you read the news you'll encounter not just information, but the people who make it. You'll find emotion, opinion, sarcasm, humor and many other human qualities—good and bad—in ample supply throughout Net News postings.

You may encounter postings on the USENET that you find offensive. You may also discover that someone else has taken offense at something you've posted. There are a few precautions that anyone can take to avoid either giving or taking offense:

- Direct your postings to the most appropriate newsgroup. If you want to make a statement about abortion, for example, make it in the `talk.abortion` newsgroup.

- Unsubscribe from newsgroups that you feel might be offensive. In addition to the unsubscribe feature, most news readers also support a "kill" facility that can be used to filter topics by keyword.

- If you must post something that is in questionable taste, state up front that the posting may not be suitable for everyone and take the additional precaution of encoding the offensive material. (See the accompanying sidebar for a description of rot13 encoding.)

ROT13 ENCODING

Rot13 is a simple encryption formula that is used in some USENET groups (`rec.humor`, for example) to encode postings that some readers might find offensive. In rot13 coding, each letter is replaced by the letter 13 farther along in the alphabet. (A becomes N, B becomes O, and so on.) Here is a string of regular text and its rot13 equivalent:

```
Passwords are like underwear, both should be changed often.
Cnffjbeqf ner yvxr haqrejrne, obgu fubhyq or punatrq bsgra.
```

Many news readers include commands to read and write rot13-encrypted text. If your news reader doesn't do rot13 coding, you can use the UNIX `tr` command to translate. This is the command to translate normal text into rot13 format:

```
tr A-Za-z N-ZA-Mn-za-m
```

Because Net News discussions take place between people who may never meet face to face, it is easy to forget that your on-line behavior has an effect on other users. A little common sense and a few rules of basic courtesy can do a lot to make the experience of using USENET more enjoyable. The following sidebar summarizes the basics of courtesy and common sense on USENET. This summary was taken from the USENET Primer, which discusses USENET etiquette more fully. The USENET Primer is regularly re-posted to the newsgroups news.answers and news.announce.newusers.so.

SUMMARY OF USENET ETIQUETTE

- Never forget that the person on the other side is human.
- Don't blame system admins for their users' behavior.
- Be careful what you say about others.
- Be brief.
- Your postings reflect upon you; be proud of them.
- Use descriptive titles.
- Think about your audience.
- Be careful with humor and sarcasm.
- Only post a message once.
- Please rotate (rot13-encrypt) material with questionable content.
- Summarize what you are following up.
- Use mail, don't post a follow-up.
- Read all follow-ups and don't repeat what has already been said.
- Double-check follow-up newsgroups and distributions.
- Be careful about copyrights and licenses.

- Cite appropriate references.

- When summarizing, summarize.

- Mark or rotate answers or spoilers.

- Spelling flames considered harmful. (English translation: Don't overreact to spelling errors.)

- Don't overdo signatures.

- Limit line length and avoid control characters.

Where to Go from Here

You can have a lot of fun and spend a lot of time rummaging through the recreational parts of the USENET. If you know where to look, you can also use it as a reference library for hundreds of topics. There are a few key newsgroups that provide an excellent point of departure for more serious excursions into Net News. To learn more about Net News itself, visit `news.announce.newusers`, `news.misc` and `news.software.readers`. In these groups you will find periodic re-postings of and updates to the USENET Primer, the list of active newsgroups, and the Net News FAQ (Frequently Asked Questions).

The single most important newsgroup is `news.answers`. This group contains more than 800 FAQ compilations from various newsgroups. With the material in `net.answers` you can come up to speed on everything from object-oriented software design to historical costuming. When you've found an FAQ for the topic you're interested in, you'll also have a pointer to the newsgroup that produced it.

 **HUNTING THROUGH THE INTERNET**

Question 1   Is this year's peanut crop larger or smaller than last year's?

Answer   On Yanoff's list, there are several sources for agricultural information. Use `telnet` to connect to one of these:

```
% telnet caticsuf.csufresno.edu
```

This connects you with the ATI-NET Bulletin Board at California State University in Fresno. The main menu for ATI-NET includes an item for Daily Agricultural Market Reports. When you select that item, a menu of Commodity Reports will appear, and one option on this menu is Statistical Reports. From this menu, select the Fruit and Vegetable Statistics, and you'll see a lengthy report that begins with a Crop Production Narrative. The narrative for peanuts is near the top of this file, and compares this year's production with last year's.

Question 2   Where can you get cricket scores?

Answer   Cricket has an avid following on the Internet. To get started, look at the `rec.cricket.scores` newsgroup. You'll get reports of scores, and pointers to other sources of cricket info, such as the CricInfo Gopher. Notice that a `veronica` search on the word "cricket" turns up five pages of menu items, many of which refer to a graphing program named `cricket`. Looking for the newsgroup first is actually a more efficient way of finding the sources you want.

APPENDIX

Internet
Resources
Directory

Lists of Internet access providers are available on the Internet itself. Use ftp to connect to is.internic.net. Information about access providers can be found in the directory getting-started/getting-connected.

US Internet Access Providers

NAME (SERVICE AREA)	PHONE NUMBER	E-MAIL ADDRESS
Alternet (US and International)	(800) 4UUNET3	alternet-info @uunet.uu.net
ANS (US and International)	(313) 663-7610	info@ans.net
BARRNet (Northern/Central California)	(415) 723-7520	info@nic.barrnet.net
CERFnet (Western US and International)	(800) 876-2373	help@cerf.net

NAME (SERVICE AREA)	PHONE NUMBER	E-MAIL ADDRESS
CICnet (Midwest US)	(313) 998-6102	hankins@cic.net
CO Supernet (Colorado)	(303) 273-3471	kharmon@csn.org
CONCERT (North Carolina)	(919) 248-1404	jrr@concert.net
International Connections Manager (International)	(703) 904-2230	rcollet@icm1.icp.net
INet (Indiana)	(812) 855-4240	ellis @ucs.indiana.edu
JVNCnet (US and International)	(800) 35TIGER	market@jvnc.net
Los Nettos (Los Angeles, CA)	(310) 822-1511	los-nettos-request @isi.edu
MichNet/Merit (Michigan)	(313) 764-9430	jogden@merit.edu
MIDnet (NE, OK, AR, MO, IA, KS, SD)	(402) 472-5032	dmf@westie.unl.edu
MRnet (Minnesota)	(612) 342-2570	dfazio@mr.net

NAME (SERVICE AREA)	PHONE NUMBER	E-MAIL ADDRESS
MSEN (Michigan)	(313) 998-4562	info@msen.com
NEARnet (ME, NH, VT, CT, RI, MA)	(617) 873-8730	nearnet-join @nic.near.net
NETCOM (California)	(408) 554-8649	info@netcom.com
netILLINOIS (Illinois)	(309) 677-3100	joel @bradley.bradley.edu
NevadaNet (Nevada)	(702) 784-6133	zitter@nevada.edu
NorthwestNet (WA, OR, ID, MT, ND, WY, AK)	(206) 562-3000	ehood@nwnet.net
NYSERnet (New York)	(315) 443-4120	info@nysernet.org
OARnet (Ohio)	(614) 292-8100	alison@oar.net
PACCOM (Hawaii and the Pacific)	(808) 956-3499	torben@hawaii.edu
PREPnet (Pennsylvania)	(412) 268-7870	twb+@andrew.cmu.edu
PSCNET (PA, OH, WV)	(412) 268-4960	pscnet-admin@psc.edu

NAME (SERVICE AREA)	PHONE NUMBER	E-MAIL ADDRESS
PSINet (US and International)	(800) 82PSI82	info@psi.com
SDSCnet (San Diego Area)	(619) 534-5043	loveep@sds.sdsc.edu
Sesquinet (Texas)	(713) 527-4988	farrell@rice.edu
SprintLink (US and International)	(703) 904-2230	bdoyle@icm1.icp.net
SURAnet (Southeastern US)	(301) 982-4600	marketing@sura.net
THEnet (Texas)	(512) 471-3241	green@utexas.edu
VERnet (Virginia)	(804) 924-0616	jaj@virginia.edu
Westnet (AZ, CO, ID, NM, UT, WY)	(303) 491-7260	pburns @yuma.acns.colostate .edu
WiscNet (Wisconsin)	(608) 262-8874	tad@cs.wisc.edu
World dot Net (OR, WA, ID)	(206) 576-7147	info@world.net
WVNET (West Virginia)	(304) 293-5192	cc011041 @wvnvms.wvnet.edu

Canadian Internet Providers

NAME (Service Area)	Phone Number	E-Mail Address
ARnet (Alberta)	(403) 450-5187	neilson@TITAN.arc.ab.ca
BCnet (British Columbia	(604) 822-3932	Mike_Patterson@mtsg.ubc.ca
MBnet (Manitoba)	(204) 474-8230	miller@ccm.UManitoba.ca
NB*net (New Brunswick)	(506) 453-4573	DGM@unb.ca
NLnet (Newfoundland and Labrador)	(709) 737-8329	wilf@kean.ucs.mun.ca
NSTN (Nova Scotia)	(902) 468-NSTN	martinea@hawk.nstn.ns.ca
ONet (Ontario)	(519) 661-2151	bjerring@uwovax.uwo.ca
PEINet (Prince Edward Island)	(902) 566-0450	hancock@upei.ca
RISQ (Quebec)	(514) 340-5700	turcotte@crim.ca
SASK#net (Saskatchewan)	(306) 966-4860	jonesdc@admin.usask.ca

APPENDIX

Internet
Documentation:
RFCs

The Internet community has developed its own conventions for documentation. Topics that are of general interest to Internet users are documented in RFCs (Request for Comments). RFC authors submit their documents to an RFC editor, who reviews the document, assigns it a number, and makes the document available on-line. Once an RFC has been published and the requested comments start to arrive, if changes are required, a new RFC is generated that renders its predecessor obsolete. Both RFCs remain in circulation, however.

Many, but by no means all, RFCs address technical topics. Some RFCs are identified as For Your Information (FYI) documents discussing issues the entire Internet community needs to be aware of. Another subset of RFCs contribute to the definition of standards, and these are known as STDs.

The RFCs themselves (and an index listing RFCs by number and title) are available from many `ftp` sites, including `ftp.nisc.sri.com` (once connected, `cd` to `rfc`) and `nis.nsf.net` (`cd` to `internet/documents/rfc`).

Following is a selection of introductory RFCs:

RFC 1118   Hitchhiker's guide to the Internet.

RFC 1175   FYI on where to start: A bibliography of internetworking information.

RFC 1206   FYI on Questions and Answers: Answers to commonly asked "new Internet user" questions.

RFC 1207   FYI on Questions and Answers: Answers to commonly asked "experienced Internet user" questions.

RFC 1150   FYI on FYI: Introduction to the FYI notes.

RFC 1208.   Glossary of networking terms.

RFC 1087   Ethics and the Internet.

APPENDIX

Logging In

The first step for anyone using a UNIX computer to connect to the Internet is to log in to the UNIX system. (Before you can log in to a UNIX system, you must have arranged with the system administrator for a login account. The administrator will give you the login name and password for your account.) No matter how you get connected to a UNIX system, you'll have to log in to begin work. Logging in tells the computer who you are. Your login name (or user name) is your on-line identity. It determines what files, directories, and programs you can work with. Any files or directories you create will be stamped with this identity so you can control access to them. All login names should also be protected by a password known only to the authorized user of the login account.

At a minimum, the UNIX login prompt looks like this:

```
login:
```

The prompt may be embellished with a brief message that identifies the computer or gives you any special login instructions for that system.

In response to the login prompt, enter your login name exactly as it was assigned by your system administrator. UNIX systems are case-sensitive, so be careful about capitalization. The characters you type in response to the login prompt are echoed on the screen as you type them. If you make a mistake, you can back over the letters you've already typed one at a time by pressing the Delete key. On some systems, you may find that the Delete key doesn't backspace over mistyped entries. If this happens, you can try using the Backspace key or simply press Return at both the login: and Password: prompts. Your login attempt will fail, and you will be returned to the login prompt. When you've entered the login name correctly, press the Return key.

You should almost immediately be prompted for your password:

```
Password:
```

Enter your password. At this prompt, characters you type are not echoed. This is intentional: maintaining the privacy of your password protects your login account, the computer, and the network from unauthorized use. Even if you aren't concerned about your own account, carelessly publicizing your password could compromise the security of other users or the network itself. When you choose a password, you should avoid words (your name, for example) that are easy to guess. You should also avoid words that might occur in common word lists (like the word list used by the UNIX spelling checker). It's a good practice to mix upper- and lowercase in your password and to include at least one number. Change your password frequently. You can correct typing mistakes in your password entry by using the Delete key carefully to backspace over the mistyped letters. If you've entered your login name and password correctly, you'll be admitted to the system. What happens next depends on how the computer is configured.

After you've logged in successfully, the system may need some additional information to set up your session correctly. The most common piece of information asked for is your terminal type. Be prepared for something like this:

```
Term? (vt100)
```

This prompt asks you to enter the type of terminal you're using (or, for users connecting to the UNIX system from another computer, the type of terminal your communication software is emulating). The prompt above proposes vt100 as a default. Vt100 terminals were built by the Digital Equipment Company (DEC); but many terminals behave like vt100s, and vt100 is a common terminal emulation.

The selection of a terminal type affects the way things look on your screen. UNIX has a database of features for common terminal types, and some of the programs you run on the UNIX computer will check the terminal type you set and try to use features of that terminal. They do this by sending control codes the terminal recognizes. If the terminal type is set correctly, these control codes will do things like clear the screen, position the cursor, or turn special video attributes on or off. If the terminal type is not set correctly, your display be difficult to work with.

If you know what sort of terminal you're emulating, enter an identifier for that terminal. Unfortunately, there is no universally appropriate response to the question about terminal type. On many systems the names "dumb" or "dialup" can be used to select a minimally featured terminal type that can be used safely.

Once you're past the login procedure and have specified a terminal type, you will receive a prompt from the UNIX command interpreter (or "shell"). Exactly what the shell prompt is depends on which UNIX shell you use and how it is configured. The shell prompt can be something simple like a "$" (the default prompt for the Bourne Shell) or a "%" (the default prompt for the C Shell). Some Internet access providers use programs other than the standard command-line interpreters for a shell program.

A Word about Terminal Servers

In some cases, particularly if you're connecting via modem, the first piece of equipment you interact with may be a terminal server and not an Internet host. A terminal server is a special-purpose computer that does nothing but manage connections between terminals or modems and the computers on a local network. When you connect to a terminal server you should see a message identifying the terminal server and brief instructions. Typically the first prompt to which you must respond is a request for a user name. In the example below, the user name for the terminal server is the same as the UNIX login name. For some systems the name you use for the terminal server may be different from your UNIX login name.

```
CONNECT 9600

                    Welcome to the Xyplex Terminal Server.


Enter username> bennett
XYRMT-7> c optimism
Xyplex -010- Session 1 to OPTIMISM established

SunOS UNIX (optimism)

login: bennett
Password:
Last login: Fri Sep 3 10:37:44 from yoda
%
```

Terminal servers are not usually protected with a password. After you've entered a username, the terminal server will start a session for you, and you can issue commands to the terminal server to start a login session with a host. You'll need to know the name of the host that you're authorized to log into. In the example above, the host was named "optimism," and the command c optimism made a connection to that computer so the user bennett could log in. Terminal servers

recognize only a few commands. Most terminal servers include a help command that you can execute by typing help, h, or ?.

What Can Go Wrong?

There are only a few ways the login procedure can misfire. By far the most common is that the login name or password is entered incorrectly. When this happens, you'll see a "Login incorrect" message and be returned to the login prompt to begin again. Different systems respond to login failures in different ways, and you should read carefully any messages or instructions that are displayed after a login attempt fails. At any point you can interrupt the login procedure and start again by typing Ctrl-D.

Occasionally during the login procedure, the computer may decide that you're on a terminal that can't distinguish between uppercase and lowercase. When this happens, everything displayed by the computer will be uppercase, and letters that ought to be capitalized will be accompanied by a "\". Here's an example of this type of login sequence:

```
IBM AIX Version 3 for RISC System/6000
(C) Copyrights by IBM and by others 1982, 1991.
login: BENNETT
3004-030 YOU LOGGED IN USING ALL UPPERCASE CHARACTERS.
        IF YOUR WORKSTATION ALSO SUPPORTS LOWERCASE
        CHARACTERS, LOG OFF, THEN LOG IN AGAIN USING
        LOWERCASE CHARACTERS.
\B\E\N\N\E\T\T'S \PASSWORD:
3004-007 \YOU ENTERED AN INVALID LOGIN NAME OR PASSWORD.
```

In this situation, the system may have difficulty recognizing your login name or password. You can use Ctrl-D to recycle the login procedure and start again. On some systems you may be able to log in successfully even when the login program thinks you're on an uppercase-only terminal. When this happens, the system will continue to display everything in uppercase, using a "\" to introduce characters that really are capitalized. Once past the login procedure you can recover from this. In response to a shell prompt, type the command:

```
% STTY -LCASE
```

This lets the system know that your terminal can handle upper- and lowercase characters, and mixed case will be used from that point on.

Just Enough
UNIX

So many of the computers on the Internet are UNIX systems that it is a real boon to be familiar with some of the basics of UNIX, even if the computer you work with directly is not a UNIX system (for example, if your Internet access is through a dial-up service that uses UNIX computers). UNIX is a multiuser, multitasking operating system developed twenty-five years ago at Bell Laboratories. Many of the design features of the original UNIX systems are still present in today's versions.

The elements of UNIX that most affect users are its file system (a collection of files and directories organized in a tree-like structure) and its operating environment.

The UNIX File System

The UNIX directory hierarchy is a tree-shaped structure that allows users to refer to any directory or file on any disk without having to know which disk contains the directory or file. (Many other operating systems, including DOS, organize their file systems hierarchically.) The entire file system is a series of directory paths that branch off from a "root" directory. Directories can contain files or other directories, and the names of directories can be strung together to form pathnames. To refer to the root directory in a command, use a slash character (/) by itself. If the / occurs at the beginning of a pathname, it is a reference to the root directory, and pathnames that begin with / are called *absolute* pathnames. The / character is also used in pathnames as a separator for directory or file names. Here are some sample absolute pathnames:

/	The root directory
/usr	A subdirectory of the root named usr.
/usr/bin	A subdirectory of /usr named bin.
/usr/bin/finger	The full pathname for the finger program in /usr/bin.

While you're logged in to a UNIX system, your login session has a current or working directory. By default, this is the home directory that the system administrator has allocated for your login name. During a login session you can change the working directory, but you'll always be in one directory or another throughout the session. Pathnames that don't begin with "/" are *relative* pathnames: they are interpreted in relation to your current working directory. When you're composing a relative pathname, you can use a period (.) to refer to the current directory and a double-period (..) to refer to the parent directory of the current directory.

UNIX provides many commands to manipulate files and directories. The commands you'll use most often are ls (list a directory's contents), cd (change directory), and pwd (print working directory). There are more detailed explanations of these commands at the end of this Appendix.

The UNIX Command Environment

When you log in to a UNIX system, you'll work with a command interpreter or shell program that accepts commands, executes programs for you, and manages the environment of your login session. There are three common shell programs in use on UNIX systems today: the Bourne Shell, the Korn Shell, and the C Shell. The Bourne and Korn shells are similar. The default prompt for them is $. The C Shell is different, particularly in its commands for managing the shell environment. The default C Shell prompt is %. Regardless of which shell you use, your login session's environment will consist of variables whose values control your access to commands and how the system behaves. By resetting these variables, you can customize your login session. Common items in the UNIX shell environment are

HOME	Full pathname for your home directory.
LOGNAME	Your login name.
MAIL	Full pathname to the file that is your system mailbox.
PATH	A list of directories that the system will search to find commands you execute.
SHELL	The default command interpreter for your login account.
TERM	The terminal type you're using.
TERMCAP	Either a description of your terminal's capabilities or a full pathname to the file containing the terminal capabilities database.

The environment variables that have the most dramatic effect on how your login session behaves are PATH and TERM. If the TERM variable is not set correctly, you may have difficulty using programs (such as terminal-based client programs for gopher or W3) that try to manipulate your screen. The PATH variable controls the list of directories that will be searched when the shell needs to look up a command for you. If you know what directory a program is stored in, you can always execute the program by typing its full pathname. For example, if the finger program is in /usr/bin, you can execute finger by typing:

```
% /usr/bin/finger rosebody@well.com
```

However, if the PATH variable in your environment includes the directory /usr/bin, you can execute finger by just typing its name:

```
% finger rosebody@well.com
```

On most UNIX systems, you can have access to everything you need with only a few directories in your path: /bin, /usr/bin, /usr/local/bin. You may also want to add /usr/etc and, if your system has it, /usr/ucb. If you're working with a commercial Internet access provider, you should not have to figure out for yourself what directories should be included in your path.

On some systems, your current directory won't be included in the PATH by default. This can be very frustrating when you try to execute a program in the current directory. The ls command shows that the program is there, but attempts to execute it by name fail with a "Command not found" message. You can execute the program by full pathname, execute it by relative pathname (./*programname*), or add the current directory to your PATH. (See the example below.)

Some application programs can be configured with environment variables as well. For example, if you want the World Wide Web line-mode browser to start up with a different home page, you can set the

WWW_HOME environment variable to indicate which page should be used.

Setting and Displaying Environment Variables

How you set environment variables depends on which shell program you use. The Bourne and Korn shells use the same syntax to set variables. For example, this is how to set the PATH variable using either of these shells:

```
$ PATH=:/bin:/usr/bin:/usr/local/bin::
$ export PATH
```

The variable is set in the first command. The export command makes the variable available to any programs you start from the session in which the variable was set. To do the same thing in the C Shell, use the setenv command:

```
% setenv PATH :/bin/usr/bin/local/bin:
```

When you're entering directory names for the PATH variable, use a colon to separate the names. If the list of directories begins with this character, your working directory will be searched first. Directories are searched in the order they appear in the PATH variable. If you want to place your current directory elsewhere in the PATH variable, use :.: at the proper location. For example, Bourne shell users can put the current directory at the end of the PATH with this command:

```
$ PATH=:/bin:/usr/bin:/usr/local/bin:.:
$ export PATH
```

With the Bourne or Korn shells, the set command can be used to display all the variables in your environment. C shell users should use the command printenv. To examine the value of only one variable, use the echo command. For example, this command displays the current PATH setting:

```
$ echo $PATH
:/usr/local/bin:/usr/ucb:/bin:/usr/bin:
```

When a variable name is preceded by a "$", UNIX substitutes the current value of the variable. The same convention is used for all the shells.

Sixteen UNIX Commands You Should Know

By design, UNIX systems use a large number of single-purpose commands. Here are brief summaries of sixteen of the most commonly used UNIX utilities. Some of the following commands require filenames or directory names on the command line. (Anything following the name of a UNIX command on the command line is called a command line "argument.") For many UNIX commands, arguments are optional. In the commands that follow, optional arguments are indicated in square brackets, with an indication of what sort of argument is expected. For example, an optional file name argument is shown as [*filename*].

`cat` *filename*

Display the named file on the screen. Similar to the DOS TYPE command.

`cd` [*pathname*]

Change the working directory to the named directory or to the user's home directory if *pathname* is omitted.

```
compress filename
compress -d filename
```

Compress (or, with the -d option, decompress) the named file. The compressed file is named *filename*.Z, and will be one-third to one-half the size of the source file. Compressed files are binary and should be passed through uuencode before being sent via mail. The decompress option looks for `filename.Z`, decompresses it, and replaces it with `filename`.

```
cp filename newname
```

Make a copy of a file. If *newname* is a directory, a copy of the file will be placed in that directory.

```
grep pattern file
```

Display any lines in the named *file* that contain the specified *pattern*.

```
head filename
```

Display the first few lines of a file.

```
ls [pathname]
```

List the contents of the named directory or the current directory if *pathname* is omitted.

```
mkdir dirname
```

Create a directory with the specified name.

```
mv oldname newname
```

Rename a file, or if *newname* is a directory, move the file to that directory.

```
passwd
```

Change your password.

pwd

Print the name of the current working directory.

rm *filename*

Remove the named file. Be careful; there is no way to "undo" the effects of rm.

rmdir *dirname*

Remove the named directory. The directory must be empty.

tail *filename*

Display the last few lines of a file.

uuencode *filename* < *filename* > *filename*.uue
uudecode *filename*.uue

Convert binary files into and out of an ASCII format that can safely be sent through programs (mail, for example) that are not intended to handle binary data.

who

List currently logged-in users.

For a full explanation of these commands, use the UNIX on-line manual. For example, to see the on-line article about the ls command type man ls.

Index

Note: Page numbers in **boldface** are a major source of information on a topic; page numbers in *italics* are references to figures.

T

E-mail Addressing between Networks (continued)

SprintMail: To send mail from a SprintMail site to an Internet user, use the following address form:

```
C:USA, A:telemail, P:internet, ID:user(a)host.domain
```

To send mail from an Internet user to a SprintMail site, use the following address form:

```
/PN=Bennett.Falk/O=co.wsqpd/ADMD=SprintMail/C=US@sprint.com
```

UUCP: To send mail from a UUCP site to an Internet user, use one of the following address forms:

```
user@host
```

or

```
gateway!domain!user
```

To send mail from an Internet user to a UUCP site, use the following address form:

```
user%host.UUCP@uunet.uu.net
```

Locating Archie Servers

Archie, discussed in Chapter 3, is a database (updated monthly) containing directory listings of what is available through anonymous `ftp` at several hundred Internet sites. The following servers host the `archie` database:

`archie.ans.net`	(USA [NY])	`archie.wide.ad.jp`	(Japan)
		`archie.ncu.edu.tw`	(Taiwan)
`archie.rutgers.edu`	(USA [NJ])	`archie.cs.huji.ac.il`	(Israel)
`archie.sura.net`	(USA [MD])	`archie.sogang.ac.kr`	(Korea)
`archie.unl.edu`	(USA [NE])	`archie.nz`	(New Zealand)
`archie.mcgill.ca`	(Canada)	`archie.kuis.kyoto-u.ac.jp`	(Japan)
`archie.funet.fi`	(Finland/ Mainland Europe)	`archie.th-darmstadt.de`	(Germany)
`archie.au`	(Australia)	`archie.luth.se`	(Sweden)
`archie.doc.ic.ac.uk`	(Great Britain/ Ireland)		